ON DISTANT SHORE

Part 3

June 4, 2016 - Sept. 4, 2016
In descending order

Val G. Abelgas

Published and printed

by TATAY JOBO ELIZES.
Self-Publisher
in 2017, under the
permission and authorization
of VAL G. ABELGAS,
author and owner of the copyright to this book. The copyright owner can withdraw this permission at his discretion without any objection from Talay Jobo Elizes at any time. Printing of this book is using the present day method of Print-On-Demand (POD) system, where prints will never run out of copies to be available for posterity. The copyright owner is free to republish with other publishers anytime.

ISBN - 13: 978 - 1976376207
ISBN - 10: 1976376203

Contact: job_elizes@yahoo.com
Website: http://tinyurl.com/mj76ccq

Special Note

Articles are arranged in reversed chronology descending from newer dates to older dates

About the author

VAL G. ABELGAS
Publisher-Editor, Philippine Post
Editor, www.thepinoyweekly.com
Columnist, On Distant Shore
valabelgas@aol.com

Val G. Abelgas, Publisher and Editor-in-Chief of the Los Angeles-based Philippine Post, has been a professional journalist for almost 45 years, 20 of them in Manila and 25 years in Los Angeles.

Val started as a sportswriter in the now defunct Philippine Daily Express in 1972 while still in his junior year in journalism at the University of the Philippines' Institute of Mass Communications. He rose to become city editor of then the country's biggest daily newspaper at a very young age of 24. He was the last managing editor of the Daily Express, which was closed down by the Cory Aquino administration in 1987. The next day, he moved to the Manila Standard as its first managing editor.

After stints as editorial consultant of the Philippine Star Group and later managing editor of the Philippine Times Journal, he and his family immigrated in 1991 to the United States, where he later obtained his green card as an alien of extraordinary ability in the field of journalism. In his first year in the US, he was editor of the Los Angeles Monitor and the next year became the first editor-in-chief of Balita. He moved to the Philippine Times in 1993, during which time he won the Newspaper of the Year and Columnist of the Year awards of the Philippine Press Club of America for two straight years in 1993 and 1994. In November 1993, he organized the first-ever nationwide convention of Filipino-American editors in Los Angeles with President Fidel V. Ramos as guest speaker. In 1995, he left the Philippine Times to join his wife Marisse in editing the Philippine Post and later became editor of Ang Peryodiko, the Pinoy Weekly and the Philippine Tribune. He published and edited two magazines with his wife, the Philippine Post Magazine and the Hiyas Magazine.

Before becoming a professional journalist, Abelgas was editor-in-chief of The Nucleus, official organ of the Manila Science High School, assistant news editor of the Philippine Collegian, official newspaper of the University of the Philippines, and editor-in-chief of the Campus Journal, laboratory newspaper of the UP-IMC.

Abelgas wrote a column, "As We See It," for the Philippines Daily Express in the 1980s. In 1992, he started writing his weekly "On Distant Shore" column, which is being published in 9 Filipino publications in the US and Canada.

Val has won numerous journalism awards both as a professional and campus journalist and served as director of the National Press Club of the Philippines five times and president of the Philippine Press Club of America. In 2016, he was named Journalist of the Year by the Filipino-American Press Club of California. He has travelled to more than 30 countries in official assignments as a journalist.

ooooo

Contents

1
Time to go nuclear
September 4, 2016

IT IS GOOD to know that the current administration is considering reviving the mothballed 620-megawatt Bataan Nuclear Power Plant (BNPP) as an option to ensure that the country would have more reliable power source to meet the demands of a booming economy and an ever-growing population.

Energy Secretary Alfonso Cusi told a Senate hearing on Tuesday that the Department of Energy has started a study on the possibility of reopening the 30-year-old nuclear plant in Morong, Bataan.

The country's power plants are few and old. Most of the time, they break down and with the working plants' reserve power very thin, intermittent brownouts have become a common occurrence, especially during the summer season when the dams are not supplying enough for power generation, and offices and homes are using more electricity.

The power needs of Luzon alone have increased by 47 percent since 2001, from 5,646 megawatts to 8,300 MW. The only one power plant that has been built since, the GN Power in Mariveles, generates only 495 MW.

As a result, the Philippines has the highest price of electricity in Asia, replacing Japan. An October 2010 study by the International Energy Consultants showed that the average retail rate of electricity in the Philippines was $0.181 per kilowatt hour as against $0.179 per kwh in Japan.

In 2010, a factory in the Philippines likely paid more than twice as much for power than a factory in Indonesia and Vietnam, and almost twice as much as a factory in Malaysia and Thailand, according to the Association of Filipino Franchisors Inc. (AFFI).

A report by Enerdata noted that in the 1990s, the Philippines' foreign direct investments were at the same level as fellow emerging economies Thailand, Indonesia and Malaysia, and 25 years later, it stayed at a level of US$1.5billion per year while the other three countries' FDI went up to between US$7 billion per year to US$18 billion per year.

The country's failure to attract more foreign direct investments can obviously be partly blamed on the excessively high electricity costs and the uncertainty of power supply.

For all his faults, the late President Ferdinand Marcos saw the need for new sources of energy other than those generated by plants fueled by oil, whose prices continued soaring and whose availability in the future were suspect. He built dams and built hydroelectric power plants. He utilized geothermal power and built geothermal power plants. Finally, he built the Bataan Nuclear Power Plant, which, unfortunately, was haunted by corruption and was closed even before it could generate a single watt of electricity.

While there are laudable efforts to find alternative sources of energy, such as putting up windmills to harness the power of the wind, putting up solar panels to harness the energy from the sun, and putting up ethanol plants to produce fuel from sugar, corn and other agricultural products, we all know that these alternative sources of energy cannot even come close to the amount of power produced by turbines using oil or coal.

And yet, we all know that in time, the world has to turn to other sources of energy because oil and coal are so expensive, their supply is seriously depleting, and they have caused so much harm to the earth's atmosphere, resulting in alarming weather phenomena such as global warming, El Nino and El Nina, drought and many other global problems.

Nuclear energy is the only viable alternative to oil-fueled and coal-fueled power. Nuclear plants can produce significant quantities of electricity, and are generally comparable in output to coal plants. There is no need to worry about interruptions to the power supply: as long as there is uranium, there will be power. While there are some greenhouse gas emissions associated with the life cycle of uranium, as gases are emitted as it is mined and transported, this is significantly less than the emissions associated with the burning of fossil fuels. Nuclear power would be "carbon-zero" if the uranium were mined and transported in a more efficient way.

More importantly, the cost of electricity will be greatly reduced and the supply uninterrupted.

According to Wikipedia, there are 434 operable nuclear plants in the world, 53 more under construction, and 432 either planned or proposed.

The United States is the biggest producer of nuclear energy with 104 operable nuclear plants, another one under construction, and 30 more planned or proposed. France is next with 59 existing plants, followed by Japan, 53 operable, 2 under construction, and 13 planned; Russia, 31 existing, nine under construction; South Korea, 20 existing, six under construction; United Kingdom, 19 existing; Canada, 18; India, 17 existing, 6 under construction and 23 more planned; Germany, 17 existing; Ukraine, 15 existing; South Korea, 20 existing, 6 under construction and 6 more planned; China, 11 existing, 18 under construction and 125 planned or proposed; and Taiwan, 6 existing and 2 more under construction.

A cursory glance of this list would reveal that these countries are among the richest and most industrialized in the world. The emerging economies have also joined the bandwagon – Thailand, which is planning to build two plants, with four more proposed; Indonesia, planning to build two and also four more proposed; Vietnam, planning to build two plants with eight more proposed; and United Arab Emirates, planning to build three with 11 more proposed.

This list alone should tell us that nuclear energy is the way to go in the future, and that the Philippines should no longer hesitate to come to grips with this reality.

Cusi has apparently come to grips with this reality.

"Coal and fuel has a lifespan. Nuclear power has

a longer life, so we will have a more secure [supply]. The hard fact is that we know that nuclear power is not popular, but it is our responsibility to look at it and study it for nation-building," he said.

Amen to that.

Ooooo

2
Alvarez gets ball rolling for Con-Com with draft EO

September 1, 2016

MANILA — Speaker Pantaleon Alvarez said he has submitted to President Rodrigo Duterte his proposed draft of an executive order (EO) forming a constitutional commission (Con-Com) that would help Congress craft a revised charter.

In his keynote speech at the membership meeting of the Philconsa Tuesday night, Alvarez said he had submitted the draft to Malacañang Tuesday afternoon.

"This afternoon I forwarded the draft of the Executive Order to the Office of the President creating the Constitutional Commission," Alvarez said Tuesday.

Alvarez said he hoped President Duterte would be able to sign the executive order by

September and appoint members of the Con-Com, so that it could start its work by October.

After Con-Com drafts a revised charter for six months, Congress can convene into a constituent assembly.

"So by October the Constitutional Commission will start their work to draft the revised Charter and perhaps in six-month's time we also–if we are able to finish the 2017 national budget—we can already convene both Houses of Congress into a Constituent Assembly where the draft will be presented by the members of the Constitutional Commission for further deliberations and debate," Alvarez said.

Ooooo

3
The saga of Jun Lozada continues
September 1, 2016

HE WAS in tears when he first surfaced in the Philippines' national consciousness. It was 2 a.m. of Feb. 7, 2008 when Rodolfo "Jun" Lozada Jr. appeared in a hastily called press conference at the De La Salle Greenhills to reveal that he had been kidnapped at the airport upon his arrival from Hongkong by police officials, and that he believed persons close to Malacanang were behind his abduction.

Lozada also said that the abduction apparently had something to do with the information he had about the controversial $320-million NTN-ZTE broadband deal. Malacanang officials were said to have panicked and feared that Lozada would appear later that day before the Senate, which was investigating the contract.

Lozada told media men that police officials took him from the airport on Feb. 5, and drove him around Laguna and Libis, during which time he said he feared for his life. He was later brought to De la Salle Greenhills in Mandaluyong, where the sisters of the Association of Major Religious Superiors of the Philippines (AMRSP) and the La Salle Brothers protected him and his family for years.

Lozada, who was then consultant to the NEDA and a friend of then NEDA chief Romulo Neri, had been invited by the Senate to shed light on the severely overpriced broadband deal. Lozada was the NEDA consultant who was tasked to review the contract, which was allegedly brokered by then Commission on Elections Chairman Benjamin Abalos and Mike Arroyo, the presidential husband. Lozada was sent to Hongkong with P500,000 shopping money apparently to evade the Senate investigation.

In his early morning press conference, Lozada gave out a handwritten outline, wherein he narrated the chronology of his involvement in the broadband project, and corroborated losing bidder and whistleblower Joey de Venecia III's previous testimonies. He also named and recounted how former election chairman

Benjamin Abalos and First Gentleman Mike Arroyo were involved in the project.

Later in the Senate, Lozada corroborated the prior testimony of Neri that Abalos had offered P200 million for the approval of the $330-million broadband project that was later canceled by President Gloria Arroyo. Lozada also testified that when Abalos had suspected a "double-cross," He said Abalos threatened to have him killed should he show up at Wack Wack or Mandaluyong City. Lozada had insisted that Abalos was trying to protect his $130-million commission from the broadband deal.

Soon after, Lozada's troubles began. He feared for his life and those of his wife and young children, and they all had to live within the confines of De Las Salle Greenhills, putting an end to normalcy in their lives. He could not work and his children could not live the way ordinary children lived.

He was charged with all kinds of crimes. Perjury charges were filed against him and his wife. The Ombudsman suddenly investigated malversation and graft cases against him. The malversation charge was in connection with the P19.6-million fund supposedly intended for the jathropa project of the Philippine Forest Corp. when Lozada was its president. The graft case involved the allegedly anomalous purchase of motor vehicles, fencing materials and other equipment worth P15 million.

In his last press conference after charges against him were given credence by the court, Lozada was exasperated: "Our lives were disrupted completely. My only hope is that our sacrifices will not be in vain."

It was obviously in vain as nobody has been convicted in the NBN-ZTE scandal after the Supreme Court dismissed all three petitions as being moot with the cancellation of the project by Arroyo.

Last week, Sandiganbayan convicted him and his brother Jose Orlando Lozada of conflict of interest and partiality for granting separate leasehold rights over public lands to his brother Jose Orlando Lozada and a private company when he headed the government-owned Philippine Forest Corp. They were sentenced to six to 10 years imprisonment.

After Lozada's conviction, the Catholic Bishops' Conference of the Philippines (CBCP) urged Congress to pass the Whistleblower Protection Act amid the administration's intensified anticorruption campaign.

The proposed bill seeks to aid in the prosecution of corrupt and erring public officials and employees through the provision of protection and reward for whistle blowers. It proposes to create a Whistleblower Protection Council that shall evaluate the qualification of whistleblowers and administer the provision of benefits and protection for them. Rewards of up to P400,000 plus 10% of any amount recovered will be provided to whistle blowers. It also grants whistleblowers immunity from liability for disclosures made under this bill, which is gathering dust in Congress.

How many times have whistleblowers like Lozada gone through similar sacrifices only to end up with shattered lives or dead, while the perpetrators of the exposed deals continue to wallow in wealth and power? And what have their sacrifices gained? Nothing. Absolutely nothing. Because the people don't seem to care, or are too numbed to do something about the abuses and injustices brought upon them.

Lozada's case is certainly not the first time that ordinary people who found courage to expose anomalies in the government had suffered the consequences. The more prominent among them were Marlene Esperat, the 45-year-old journalist who was the first to expose the P720-million fertilizer scam, and Siche Bustamante-Gandinao, who boldly testified before the Alston Commission on the killing of her father-in-law, Dalmacio Gandinao, a member of the militant Misamis Oriental Farmers Association.

Esperat was shot on Maundy Thursday in 2005 while eating dinner with her 10-year-old son inside her house in Sultan Kudarat. It turned out later that high-ranking officials of the Department of Agriculture had tried to talk Esperat into withdrawing the charges she had filed against agriculture officials a few days before she was killed. The Esperat expose later turned out to be just the tip of the iceberg that was to be infamously known as the P760-million fertilizer scam, where hundreds of millions of government funds earmarked for fertilizer subsidies for farmers were allegedly diverted to Arroyo's campaign funds.

Siche Gandencio, on the other hand, was shot dead in front of her family in Misamis

Oriental in 2006, just a week after United Nations rapporteur Philip Alston had left Manila after completing an investigation of the unsolved political killings in the Philippines. Gandencio was one of the few relatives of political slay victims who testified before the Alston Commission.

And in 2007, Musa Dimasidsing, the courageous Maguindanao school district supervisor who exposed election anomalies in that same province that was prominently involved in the 2004 Hello Garci poll fraud, was murdered. Dimasidsing had revealed that gunmen filled up ballots or made teachers fill them up with names of Team Unity senatorial candidates while guns were pointed at them.

The bigger tragedy was that all these three people who chose courage over their personal safety and comfort died in vain! All their sacrifices went to naught as the perpetrators of the corruption and abuses that they dared expose remain free.

Lozada now faces the prospect of jail. And his life and those of his family will never be the same again. For many years, they have suffered through it all, but he never backtracked. He never gave up. It was the people – for whom he had offered his life and from whom he had expected support – who gave up on him.

Ooooo

4
Looking after our own
August 24, 2016

SOME minority groups are doing well in business because they take care of their own. Among these groups are the Koreans, Japanese, Chinese, Armenians, and Indians. If these people need to purchase something, they first look in their compatriots' stores and if the prices were competitive, they would buy from their fellow countrymen. If they need workers, they would first look for compatriots who would meet their basic requirements before even trying other applicants.

In other words, these people would first look inside their backyard before going out to search in other backyards. For example, if a Korean restaurant owner needs meat and vegetables, he would first check if there's a Korean supplier and if that supplier's prices are competitive with other suppliers. If that same restaurant owner needs waitresses, he would advertise first in Korean newspapers to look for Korean applicants. If that same restaurant owner needs additional financing, he would go to a Korean bank and most probably, that Korean bank would do its best to grant the business owner's loan request.

It is unfortunate that while Filipino families do look after their own, such patronizing attitude is often not carried by Filipinos outside their close family. More often than not, Filipinos tend to keep an arm's length from Filipino businessmen and professionals.

It is that innate distrust for fellow Filipinos that has helped to prevent unity among Filipinos, and consequently, hamper better political and economic opportunities for Filipinos in America.

A Filipino old-timer would, for example, caution friends and family who have just arrived in the United States to beware of fellow Filipinos. They would say many Filipinos are "mandaraya" (cheaters) or "manloloko" (con artists). Many Filipinos are inclined to believe this myth, and would, thus, keep away from fellow Filipinos when conducting business.

For example, a Filipino needing an attorney to represent him in an accident litigation or in his immigration case would rather go to a non-Filipino lawyer, because he fears that Filipino lawyers would just cheat him of his hard-earned money, or he is worried that a Filipino lawyer would have no chance before an American jury or American INS officers.

This, of course, is farthest from the truth. Filipino lawyers are among the best in the world, and although there are, indeed, some unscrupulous Filipino lawyers, these are the exception rather than the rule.

A Filipino doctor, on the other hand, would rather hire a Hispanic medical assistant than a fellow Filipino for the flimsy reason that most of their clients are Hispanics. If this were the case, then all offices and businesses in California should all hire Hispanic workers because, after all, Latinos comprise a big majority of the state's population.

Why must Filipino businesses adjust to the Hispanics and speak Spanish to conduct business with them (Habla Espanol, say Filipino medical clinics)? Will Hispanic doctors hire Filipino medical assistants because most of their patients are Tagalog-speaking? Will a liquor store owned by Hispanics hire Filipino cashiers because most of their customers are Filipinos?

When they need a mechanic, how many Filipinos would go to a Filipino mechanic? When they need couriers, how many Filipino businessmen would go to a Filipino-owned courier company? When they need a contractor, how many Filipinos would look for a Filipino contractor? When they need accountants, how many Filipinos would go to a Filipino accountant?

Filipinos in America will have to learn to trust their countrymen again. We will have to start looking after our own if we want to achieve economic advancement as a people. Let us patronize Filipino businesses. Let us look after our own.

Ooooo

5
Sterner warning for gun smugglers?
August 21, 2016

Almost exactly a year to the day when then President Aquino ordered a stop to the mandatory physical inspection of all balikbayan boxes in the wake of worldwide protest from overseas Filipino workers, another illegal act by some unscrupulous persons is threatening to force the Bureau of Customs to tighten the squeeze again on balikbayan box senders.

Last Thursday, Customs Commissioner Nick Faeldon said the bureau had seized high-caliber firearms illegally shipped through a balikbayan box from the United States.

The firearms, sent by a certain Maiko Claridad of California, were concealed among household items inside a balikbayan box that was taken to the warehouse of Atlas Shippers International in Covina. Somehow, the heavy box raised the suspicion of the Department of Homeland Security, which then informed the customs bureau in the Philippines that a balikbayan box containing disassembled firearms was on its way there.

Atlas Shippers fully cooperated with the Department of Homeland Security in the United States and the Bureau of Customs in the Philippines in the discovery and seizure of the firearms and the eventual arrest of the shipment's consignee.

"We will not tolerate illegal acts in the shipment of balikbayan boxes," stressed Joel P. Longares, president and CEO of the Covina-based Atlas Shippers International, in a press statement.

Customs personnel monitored the box upon arrival at the Atlas Shippers warehouse in Las Pinas up to delivery to the company's warehouse in Bacolod City on August 4. After the consignee, a certain businessman named Leo Mendietta, accompanied by an aide, Wilford Z. Palma, turned up to claim the box two days later, agents from the Criminal Investigation and Detection Group (CIDG) arrested them.

Mendietta's real name is actually Brian C. Ta-Ala, and now, he is seeking a writ of amparo with a plea for a protection order from the court. Obviously fearful for his life amid reports of police killings of drug pushers and other criminals, Ta-Ala is confined in a hospital and refusing to go to Manila for further investigation.

Found inside the box were the following items: 35 pieces trigger housing assembly, 60 pieces upper receiver, 15 pieces batter spring lock, 10 pieces barrel assembly M16, 1 piece rail without barrel, 1 piece rail w/ M16 barrel with 1 piece suppressor, 15 pieces butt assembly (10 pieces black and 5 pieces gray), 15 pieces buffer spring guide, 5 pieces quick detach sope mount, and 2 pieces bottle opener.

It was not the first time that firearms were discovered inside a balikbayan box, but it has been awhile since anybody tried to smuggle guns again through that ubiquitous box. The sender and the consignee probably haven't heard of President Duterte's aggressive campaign against drug pushers and criminals.

In 2003, Customs examiners in Manila, acting on a tip, found several high-powered firearms, handguns and ammunitions in three balikbayan boxes shipped from the United States.

The guns, wrapped in aluminum foil and covered by rubber tubes, were found concealed in big pressure cookers and speaker components. One box, shipped from Chicago, contained two .45 caliber Colt Mark IV Gold Cup pistols and one 40.9 mm Glock Series 22. Another box contained two Armotech Armalite rifles model WG-65 and three Armalite spray guns.

The third box, sent from Ohio, was found to contain a.380 caliber Bryco Arms handgun, .38 caliber Smith & Wesson, 150 bullets for .380, 420 bullets for .22 caliber handgun, 21 bullets for .38 caliber revolver, .380 handgun magazines and trigger locks.

Years back, alert Customs operatives at the Manila International Container Port in North Harbor also seized high-powered firearms and ammunition neatly concealed inside a balikbayan box and declared as personal effects.

Among the weapons seized were a .45 caliber Springfield Armory pistol, a .45 caliber Browning Arms pistol, a .40 caliber Sig Sauer pistol, a caliber 223Ruger mini 14 rifle, several magazines and thousands of ammunition. The shipment also came from the United States.

The shipper, however, was found out to be fictitious and the US address non-existent.

In April 2002, Customs agents at the Ninoy Aquino International Airport made the biggest catch of firearms, explosives and ammunition worth at least P35 million.

The cargo was packed in four balikbayan boxes and consigned to Trimark Venture Corp.

It contained 223 short handguns, high-powered state-of-the-art assault rifles, sub-machineguns, biological suits, armored vests, 1,600 pieces of magazines and bullets.

In August last year, then Customs Commissioner Alberto Lina ordered an increase in the processing fees for containers carrying balikbayan boxes and a mandatory physical inspection of all balikbayan boxes passing through customs.

The order was met with a howl of protests from overseas Filipinos who wondered whether it was the government's way of showing gratitude for their about $25 billion yearly remittances, which account for about 15 percent of the country's GDP.

After a series of Senate public hearings where affected overseas Filipino workers (OFWs), balikbayan box industry players and senators protested Lina's directives, then President Aquino ordered Lina to stop the mandatory physical inspections and suspended the increased processing fees.

And now, the reckless and illegal acts of that balikbayan box sender from California, in connivance with the unscrupulous consignee in Bacolod, are threatening to bring back rigid inspections of these boxes, which is certain to cause another round of delays in deliveries, not to mention damage or loss of certain items inside the boxes.

Maybe they need a sterner warning the same way drug dealers are being given daily under the Duterte administration?

Ooooo

6
Regaining one's cultural identity
August 16, 2016

THERE were at least two things that caught my attention while watching the latest performance of the Filipino American Symphony Orchestra (FASO) at the John Wayne Performing Arts Center in Glendale last Saturday. One was the nostalgic rendering of three kundiman songs by the "Queen of Kundiman" herself, Sylvia la Torre with her granddaughter, Disney star Ana Maria de Tagle. The other was Ana Maria, born and raised in San Francisco, speaking very fluent Tagalog and singing Tagalog songs as if it were her native tongue.

To hear "Ibyang" sing "Diyos Lamang ang Nakakaalam," "Nasaan Ka Irog," and "Bituing Marikit" to the beautiful music of a 60-piece symphony orchestra was an experience to behold because it brought us back to the 50s and 60s when my father sang kundimans (love songs) like he was serenading my mother.

The rendition made us proud and aware of our cultural heritage.

The conversation and duet in Filipino between the lola, who is 82, and the apo, who is 25, was even more adorable because August is National Language Month in the Philippines.

Let me lead you back to an article I wrote in August 2012 entitled "Language is a people's soul."

"August is National Language Month in the Philippines. But ass in previous years, it will come and go without much fanfare. This may seem unimportant for Filipinos now living in the United States. But to me, the national language reflects a people's soul.

"Some people tend to forget the importance of their native language once they set foot on foreign soil. Trying very hard to adapt to their new country, these people speak the new language however difficult it is for them.

"When you speak in English to an American who knows no other language but English, or to another person who can only communicate with you in English, that is called necessity. When you talk to a Filipino in English in the presence of other persons who only understand English, that's courtesy. But when you talk in English to a fellow Filipino in private or in the presence of fellow Filipinos who all understand Tagalog or your native tongue, that may be deemed as "TH" or trying hard to be American.

"Of course, it is every one's prerogative to speak in the language he or she wants. But it speaks volumes about how one loves his roots, his native land. How many Latinos do you hear talking to their children, friends, or neighbors in English? Not many, I'm sure. Although they and their children or their friends speak English fluently, they would still talk to each other in

Spanish, unless, of course, there are other people around who do not speak Spanish.

"Many Filipinos, in their desire to make their children speak fluent English, talk to their small kids only in English, even when they are at home. This is a carryover from their days in the Philippines. Back home, kids who speak in English are considered smart, intelligent, and most probably, children of wealthy parents. That's why when they hear their small kids growing up in America and speaking fluently in English, they feel they have reached that status they have always desired in the Philippines. Never mind if the kid forgets how to speak in Pilipino. Never mind if he doesn't understand a single Pilipino word. (Although the 1987 Constitution spells both Filipino as a person, and Filipino as a language with "F," I purposely spelled the language with "P" as a journalistic style to differentiate it from the person.)

"These parents reason out that the children might have difficulty learning the English language if they spoke to them in Pilipino, and the children have to speak in English at school. This can't be any farther from the truth. You can teach a child five languages at the same time, and he'll learn them all.

"I once met a young Filipino who just graduated from a prestigious university. He spoke very fluent English, having been born and raised in the United States. His mother, who hailed from Pampanga, spoke to him since birth only in English, and even told his friends and relatives to speak to the boy only in English.

"As a young boy, he got along very well with his young American friends. But when he went to the university and began associating with Filipino friends, that's when he began feeling sorry for himself for not learning to speak in Pilipino. His Filipino friends would all talk in Pilipino and he couldn't understand a word of what they were saying. He wanted to leave the group and join the mainstream guys, but he loved the company of his fellow Filipinos. He felt he belonged with them.

"He blamed his mother for not teaching him how to speak in Pilipino and even Kapampangan. His Filipino friends, who were not even born in the US, could speak very fluent English, and could speak and understand Pilipino, too! And some of them could even speak a third language or dialect — Ilocano, Cebuano, Kapampangan, and other Pilipino dialects.

"He felt losing his Filipino soul. But he is now trying to regain it, he said, by trying his best to speak and understand Pilipino. It's never too late to regain one's heritage and cultural identity.

Ooooo

7
Filipinos should reject Trump

August 13, 2016

I'M NOT sure if I even wanted to add my voice to the chorus of people from both sides of the political fence in denouncing Republican presidential candidate Donald Trump for his bigotry and reckless demagoguery, but with his recent attack on the Philippines and Filipinos, I know I just have to.

Trump touched the nerves of Filipinos when he lumped the Philippines with the likes of Pakistan, Afghanistan. Somalia, Morocco, Iraq, Syria, Yemen and Uzbekistan as countries whose citizens should be barred from immigrating to the United States because they could potentially be recruited into Islamic terrorist groups.

"You have no idea who they are. This could be the great Trojan horse of all time," he said, repeating his warning that terrorists, including members of the Islamic State extremist group, will sneak into the United States as refugees. This is a practice that has to stop." "We're dealing with animals," he said.

His unforgiveable attack on Filipinos exposed his unmatched duplicity because some years back, when he launched his real estate project bearing his name in Manila, he had high praises for the country: "I've always loved the Philippines. I think it is just a special place and Manila is one of Asia's most spectacular cities."

His recent remark also highlighted his ignorance of history. He has been very busy exploding tirades against Latinos and Muslims, he ignored the fact that hundreds of thousands of Filipinos lost their lives fighting side by side with Americans against the Japanese in World War II and that the some four million Filipinos in the US are contributing significantly to American economy and society.

But Filipinos are not the only ones shocked and worried by Trump's tirades. Even some ranking members of the party that nominated him have openly said they would not vote for Trump with 50 former national security officials warning he would be the "most reckless president in American history" if elected.

The group, which included former homeland security chiefs, intelligence directors, senior presidential advisors and a former US trade representative, said: "We are convinced that he would be a dangerous president and would put at risk our country's national security and well-being."

They said the brash billionaire is unfit for office, saying that Trump "lacks the character, values, and experience to be president" and displays "alarming ignorance of basic facts" of international politics. They warned that Trump's "erratic behavior" has alarmed America's closest allies and that he fails to recognize the indispensible nature of such diplomatic relationships.

Trump first showed his bigotry and racist character when early in the campaign, he called Mexico a nation that sends its illegal drug traffickers, rapists and killers as immigrants to the US. He then vowed to build a wall between the US and Mexico.

And when pressed on the cases against Trump University, Trump said Judge Gonzalo Curiel, who was handling the cases, can not effectively preside over the cases because of an "inherent conflict of interest" due to his stated call to build a wall on the United States' southern border and Curiel's Mexican heritage.

And then he turned his attention to Muslim immigrants. He said he would stop all foreign Muslims from entering the United States. Last month, Trump belittled the parents of a slain Muslim US serviceman who had strongly denounced Trump during the Democratic National Convention. The soldier's father, Trump suggested, delivered the whole speech because his mother was not allowed to speak.

Pakistani immigrant Khizr Khan galvanized the Democratic National Convention with a tribute to his dead son in which he rebuked the Republican nominee for having "sacrificed nothing" for the country.

US billionaire Warren Buffet rebuked Trump for belittling Khan's speech. "How in the world can you stand up to a couple of parents who have lost a son and talk about sacrificing because you were building a bunch of buildings?"

Buffett is one of several extremely wealthy Americans to back Clinton for president, including billionaire and independent former mayor of New York Michael Bloomberg and Dallas Mavericks owner Mark Cuban.

It is not just his fellow billionaires dumping Trump. Every time Trump opens his mouth, the list of dissatisfied Republicans who refuse to support him in the elections are growing.

I've never seen a political party divided this badly by its presidential nominee. Only last Thursday, 75 former Republican officials wrote a letter asking the Republican National Committee to divert the funds set aside for the presidential campaign to ensure that the party would keep its majority in Congress by sending funds for the Trump campaign to House and Senate candidates struggling against Democratic rivals.

If he can't unite his own party, how can anyone expect Trump to unite the whole country? In his campaign to become the president and commander-in-chief of the world's most powerful nation, he has only sown hatred, fear, anger and divisiveness.

Many ranking Republicans in both national and state levels have expressed dissatisfaction with Trump and some have even vowed not to vote for the billionaire demagogue. Even longtime Republicans, including several Filipinos, have said they cannot support Trump because he would be a dangerous president. After just a few days of blabbering and blunders, Trump's three-point lead in the polls over Democratic nominee Clinton just before their respective national conventions has turned into a 15-point margin for the former First Lady, senator and Secretary of State.

The 50 former Republican national security officials have every reason to be concerned about a Trump presidency. With the world precipitously threading on the precipice of war in various fronts, it is frightening to think that a man as imbalanced and as reckless as Trump would be holding the code and the key to the launching of nuclear missiles that could send the world to oblivion.

Filipinos should unite this time and join the only course of action available to Americans – reject Trump.

Ooooo

8
'Slippery slope toward tyranny'
August 10, 2016

AMID the relative silence that has met the deadly war against drugs launched by President Duterte since he assumed office on June 30, three female voices have stood to denounce the killings.

"I must admit, the public reaction to these executions is not in favor of those who oppose it. A 91% approval rating for the President and what he stands for is a formidable record. But we cannot base our reactions to these killings on the popularity of the President. Popular or not, MURDERS MUST STOP. S-T-O-P. STOP. Stop the killings now!" neophyte Sen. Leila De Lima said in her first privilege speech.

"There might not be a manifest public outcry, but there is definitely a seething undercurrent of remonstration against the disregard for human life," she said.

Vice President Leni Robredo, on the other hand, said she understood the government's campaign against drugs, but she was worried about the campaign's seeming diminution of the value of human life.

"Right now it's anyone's game. For the simplest reasons, people kill. That is what I am worried about, the culture of impunity and violence," Robredo said.

"I hope my being vocal against [extrajudicial killings] inspires many others to follow suit because there really has to be public outcry. The way I see it, there has been very little public outcry in the recent past," Robredo said.

Supreme Court Chief Justice Maria Lourdes Sereno cautioned judges named by Duterte not to surrender to police without an arrest warrant as she warned that "a premature announcement of an informal investigation on allegation of involvement with the drug trade will have the unwarranted effect of rendering the judge veritably useless in discharging his adjudicative role."

"Thus, this Court has been careful, all too aware that more often than not, a good reputation is the primary badge of credibility and the only legacy that many of our judges can leave behind," she said.

I've never been a fan of De Lima, but I must commend the senator for keeping the opposition alive against the culture of violence and disrespect for the rule of law that the new President has apparently set as policy for the police to push his campaign against illegal drugs.

"Due process has nothing to do with my mouth. There are no proceedings here, no lawyers," Duterte said in a pre-dawn speech just before naming 159 local officials, judges and policemen he said were involved in the illegal drug trade.

The opposition, if ever there is still one, seems to have decided to keep its silence for now as it tries to gauge the reaction of the people to the about 13-a-day murders perpetrated by the police and vigilantes supposedly in the name of law and order.

Five senators – Franklin Drilon, Grace Poe, Risa Hontiveros, Joel Villanueva and Ralph Recto – at least agreed with De Lima that "due process and the rule of law must be dutifully upheld."

Hontiveros expressed concern about the naming of the suspects publicly, saying "democracy was never about the President's absolute power to determine innocence or guilt."

"The executive cannot blacken the reputation of people and judge them at will. The responsibility falls upon our judicial system. Sadly, the President's list, while it may be motivated by good intentions, preempts the court's judgment and tears at the very fabric of our democracy," she said.

Duterte was obviously emboldened to escalate his "name and shame" policy against all sectors of society that he perceives or was made to believe were engaged in illegal drugs trade after receiving an unprecedented 91-percent popularity rating. He has also threatened to "name and shame" governors, lawmakers, businessmen, rich taxpayers, all without the benefit of due process or even the decency to check the facts before announcing them publicly.

The President's popularity should not give him a reason to trash the Constitution and pertinent laws in his apparently sincere efforts to combat crime and illegal drugs in the country. After all, we're still a country governed by laws and democratic ideals where an accused is presumed innocent until proven guilty, and where every individual, both the accuser and the accused, are entitled to due process.

The Chief Executive cannot go around warning people that they will be killed by policemen if they did not surrender – even without arrest warrant. Just recently, he threatened to kill businessmen practicing "endo" or contractualization if they did not stop the practice.

"I'm telling this to you. I'm just issuing a warning. You choose: Stop contractualization or I kill you," the President said. "You know why? I can utter things like that. I am [the] President. I have immunity. I can summon you. I will shoot you [and order] 'Bring him to the funeral parlor. You're making me angry."

"I will call you here. I'll slap you one by one. I'm used to that. I really kick people. Believe me. Even policemen in Davao. Nobody was exempted," he added.

This was the Chief Executive speaking, saying in so many words that as a President immune from suits, he can do what he pleases, including slapping and killing people on the mere suspicion of infraction and without due process. And that's what worries some people, including De Lima.

"We are already on the slippery slope toward tyranny, without martial law, when we allow one man to be judge, jury and executioner. This is just the start," De Lima said.

Even North Korea's dictator, Kim Jung-un, brings people he suspects of disloyalty or other violations to trial before executing them. And North Korea has an authoritarian government, not a democracy like the Philippines.

We do not question Duterte's sincerity in his desire to combat crime and corruption, but we have to be alarmed by his flagrant disregard for human life, the rule of law and democratic institutions in carrying it out. As they say, the road to hell is paved with good intentions.

Ooooo

9
Cha-cha: Just like the dance
August 7, 2016

THE PEOPLE have consistently rejected the idea of amending the Philippine constitution in surveys after surveys, and yet the move to amend that sacred document, in what is commonly called "cha-cha," surfaces almost year after year.

I really can't understand Filipino politicians' obsession for charter change and why the first thing that comes to their mind when a system fails is to dump it and change it, when it is obvious that it fails not because it is defective but more like those who implement it are the ones at fault.

The latest survey by Pulse Asia showed that 44 percent of Filipinos still do not want the 1987 Constitution amended as against 37 percent who favor cha-cha. Nineteen percent are undecided, and until they have decided otherwise, that should count with those not favoring charter change.

Of those who do not agree that the constitution should not be amended, 29 percent said it may be revised in the future. In other words, cha-cha is not a priority to them at this time. Fifteen percent said it should never be amended.

What is even more telling is that 73 percent of those surveyed have "little" to "no knowledge" of the Constitution. How do you expect these people to vote intelligently when an amended Constitution is submitted to them for referendum?

Sen. Vicente Sotto III, who expressed reservations about cha-cha, said it simply: "As they say, if it ain't broke, why fix it?" He said what the country needs is a different cha-cha — character change."

Indeed, how can we be so sure that changing the system would be better when it is the same politicians who will be running the new system of government? Until the ills that have plagued the government for decades — corruption, political patronage, cronyism, and many more — any kind of system is bound to fail. And then, they will call again for another charter change?

Cha-cha proponents will argue that it is precisely the system that breeds all these flaws, so it should be changed. And they want us to believe that a federal-parliamentary form of government, or whatever combination of political systems, would remove corruption, cronyism, political patronage, etc.? I am more inclined to believe that it is the other way around — that the country's political system has failed because of the people who run them.

In any case, it appears there is no turning back on the cha-cha as President Rodrigo Duterte appears hell-bent on amending the Constitution in the first half of his term. In the first place, Duterte ran on a platform of change, obviously including charter change since he has been pushing for a shift to a federal system, which would only be possible with an amendment to the constitution.

However, it is not correct to assume that since Duterte won overwhelmingly, it follows that the people approve of federalism. It is safe to assume that Duterte won because he reflected the frustration of the people at the way politicians are running the government, not because he espoused federalism, which surveys have shown people have little or no knowledge about.

With both the Senate and the House of Representatives under Duterte's control, it shouldn't be difficult to assume that there will be a cha-cha during his term, most probably in the first half of his six-year presidency. He had stated that he expects charter change to be accomplished in the first two years.

Having said that, the debate has now shifted to how the charter change would be done. There is, of course, the traditional constitutional convention, where a group of persons elected by the people in a special election will be tasked with coming up with amendments to the constitution working full time.

And there is the so-called con-ass or the constituent assembly, where the current crop of senators and congressmen sitting as one chamber will deliberate on and approve proposed charter changes.

House Speaker Pantaleon Alvarez, Duterte's chosen one in Congress, has proposed the creation of a constitutional commission, which would almost certainly be known as "con-comm" as opposed to con-con and con-ass, through an executive order.

The members of the proposed body would be appointed by the President and will come from the academe and non-governmental organizations. These people will be experts in their fields and will work full time to come up with charter changes that will be submitted to Congress for consideration.

In both the con-ass and the con-comm, the senators and congressmen will still be deliberating on it for approval and submission to the President and the people.

And there lies the problem. The House of Turncoats and the Senate, which has suddenly turned meek in the midst of Duterte's popularity, will still have the final say before submission to the people in a referendum. With just three senators comprising the minority bloc in the

Upper House and a handful of congressmen in the Lower House, is it difficult to assume that what Duterte wants, Duterte gets in an issue that will completely change the course of our country?

Still, having a con-comm before the con-ass would still be preferable to just the con-ass kicking our asses.

Suddenly, a concept that has not gained acceptance by the Filipino people could become a reality within the next six years. Will it solve the country's woes? Will it finally push us to the economic status of our Asian neighbors? Will it benefit the people? Or will it just further divide the already divided country? Will it balkanize the Philippines into different republics? Will it eventually lead to secession by Mindanao as 36 percent of Dabawenos believe it would in a survey conducted last year?

There are just too many questions that need to be answered on the issue of federalism and it should be discussed and debated by qualified and credible minds, not the traditional politicians in Congress whose principles depend on who holds the purse in Malacanang.

There are also many other proposed amendments that should be weighed by legal, social and economic experts, not by congressional members whose credibility and competency are in question.

Having said this, I favor a constitutional convention whose members will be elected on the basis of their competence to dissect, discuss and design a proposed new constitution that would be acceptable and beneficial to the people.

Duterte himself had originally said he preferred constitutional convention over a constitutional assembly. Last week, he decided it would be better to have the con-ass to deliberate non cha-cha because, he said, it would cost at least P50 billion to hold an election and provide a separate budget for the special body.

But why worry about that expense when it is the future of our country and our people at stake? We don't want a situation where the cha-cha would bear the same result as the popular dance itself – a few steps forward and a few steps backwards, leaving you in the same place where you started.

Ooooo

10
Road rage: Something has to be done
August 2, 2016

IT WAS a ghastly sight.

A biker slightly hits a small car in Quiapo. The car cuts off a man on a bicycle and an altercation ensued between the car's driver and the biker. The car's driver got off the car and confronted the biker, resulting in a fistfight. After absorbing some punches and being held by the neck, the car's driver goes back to his car where his lady companion, presumably his wife, and his four-year-old daughter were crying.

The biker held out his hand to the driver after he noticed a Philippine Army sticker on his windshield, and then walked away with his bike. Instead of just driving away, the driver gets off his car again, this time with a handgun, approached the biker and shot him close range on the head. The biker falls and the driver puts more bullets into his body.

And then the driver drove away. I can imagine how horrified his lady companion and his young daughter were. Just as horrified were at least two eyewitnesses shown on the CCTV video and a young college scholar, Rocel Bondoc, who was hit with a stray bullet that grazed her kidney. Rocel survived but had to drop out of school for at least the semester.

The driver, Vhon Martin Tanto, fled but was captured the next day in Masbate. He was presented to the media with a partially closed left eye, which he obviously got from the fistfight. His eyes will heal, but the biker, Mark Vincent Garalde, will forever be gone. Tanto's wife will have to take care of his four children, one of whom will never forget the horror that played out before her, bll because Tanto could not control his anger.

Road rage. How many have been killed and maimed in your name?

Road rage has hit the front pages a few times before. Before the Quiapo incident, five road rage incidents top the list, as enumerated by topgear.com:

1. Raul Bautista and Sowaib Salie. On June 21, a traffic altercation in Imus, Cavite turned into a deadly family feud as it left six

people dead. The trouble started at a traffic jam on the Nueno highway in Imus as Sowaib Salie repeatedly honked his vehicle's horns at the car in front–driven by Raul Bautista. A confrontation erupted when both motorists arrived at the public market. Bautista then left the scene only to come back later with reinforcement in tow. A brief firefight erupted leaving six people dead, including Bautista, his two sons and the family driver, and Salie and his fellow trader Mahmod Sultan.

2. Eldon Maguan and Rolito Go. This incident put road rage on the front page of every newspaper in the country. On July 2, 1991, 25-year-old Eldon Maguan, a De La Salle University engineering student, was driving his car down a one-way street in San Juan and nearly collided with Rolito Go's vehicle, which was traveling the wrong way. The businessman got off his car and shot Maguan, who died a few days later.

3. Feliber Andres and Inocencio Gonzales. The Andres family's 1998 All Saints' Day eve pilgrimage to the Loyola Memorial Park in Marikina took a ghastly turn when their vehicle nearly collided with the one driven by Inocencio Gonzalez. Noel Andres tailed Gonzalez' vehicle first before he cut his path which resulted in a confrontation between the two motorists. In the heat of the argument, Gonzalez pulled out a gun and shot at the Andres' vehicle, hitting Andres' pregnant wife, Feliber, their two-year old son, and their nephew. Feliber did not survive the attack but the doctors were able to save her baby. The son and the nephew were discharged from the hospital a few days later.

4. Jay Llamas. Jay Llamas was traversing the busy northbound lane of Taft Avenue on January 10, 2003 when his Toyota Corolla was bumped by a motorcycle as they neared the Buendia intersection. Llamas and the unnamed motorcycle driver got into a heated argument which ended when the suspect drew a gun and shot Llamas at close range three times–twice in the head and once in the body. The suspect then hailed a parked tricycle and fled the scene. The case remains unsolved to this date.

5. Edgardo Canizares and Manuel Hernandez Jr. On October 2, 2007, Edgardo Canizares was traveling with a passenger along Gen. Roxas Street near the corner of Shaw Boulevard when his Nissan Cefiro almost hit the car of Manuel Hernandez Jr., a Pasig City Hall legal officer and nephew of a Sandiganbayan Justice. Hernandez was reportedly driving against the flow of traffic, prompting an angry Canizares to get out of his car and insult Hernandez. Hernandez pulled out a gun and shot Canizares four times and his passenger, twice.

These are a few of the hundreds of road rage incidents that occur daily in the Philippines' streets. Many of them go unpublished because it has become a common occurrence in the country, especially in Metro Manila, where the monstrous traffic jams are enough to make motorists lose their cool.

Road rage has also become a problem in the United States, although in far less degree. The US National Highway Traffic Safety Administration suggests that many factors have potentially played a role in causing drivers to become more aggressive: an increase in traffic congestion; increasingly busy schedules causing more people to be running late; cultural disregard for others and for the law as influenced by films and television; longer commuting times; and violent video games.

In the Philippines, probably the biggest reason for road rage is the arrogant behavior of motorists who feel their having better cars or higher status in life give them the right to assault others, including motorists on the road.

California has a road rage law that provides for suspension of the driving privilege of any operator of a motor vehicle who commits an assault as described under California Penal Code Section 245(a). The target of the road rage can be an operator or passenger of another vehicle, an operator of a bicycle or a pedestrian. For a first offense, the license suspension is six months; it is one year for second or a subsequent offense, at the court's discretion. In addition to the suspension or as an alternative to it, the court also can order the person to complete an anger management or road rage course.

Penal Code Section 245(a) sets forth various punishments for assault (be it carried out with a deadly weapon, firearm or by any means likely to produce greatly bodily injury). These punishments range from state prison for two, three or four years, or in county jail for a maximum of one year and/or a fine up to $10,000. Needless to say, if the assault leads to death, the case becomes murder or manslaughter.

Sen. Bongbong Marcos has filed Senate Bill No. 2923, also known as the Road Rage Law, that aims to curb the occurrences of senseless violence on Philippine roads, and to instill discipline, control, and restraint among road users. He filed the bill on July 28, 2011 and the measure remains pending in the Committee on Public Order in the Senate.

The proposed measure imposes higher penalties and sanctions on road rage incidents especially if a deadly weapon is involved. Section 5 of the bill states that a road rage perpetrator should be penalized with life imprisonment if a victim dies.

Road rage has become a very serious problem everywhere, but most especially in the Philippines. The problem becomes even worse when at least one of those involved has a gun. Superficial wounds, sprains and black eyes heal in time, but gun wounds are often fatal, especially when shot from close range.

Congress should take a serious look at it this time.

Ooooo

11
The need for a strong opposition
July 31, 2016

TO THE victors belong the spoils. Thus, despite having only three members in the House of Representatives and one in the Senate, the

PDP-Laban has taken leadership of both chambers of Congress with Davao del Norte Rep. Pantaleon Alvarez becoming Speaker of the House and Sen. Aquilino "Koko" Pimentel III elected as Senate President.

Pimentel, the president of the PDP-Laban party that fielded eventual winner Davao City Mayor Rodrigo Duterte as its presidential candidate, got 20 out of 24 votes to win the Senate presidency, a post his distinguished father, Sen. Aquilino "Nene" Pimentel Jr. also held.

Alvarez, a returning congressman who has been credited as the one who prodded Duterte to run for president, garnered 251 votes in an overwhelming victory over Ifugao Rep. Teddy Baguilat, who got 8 votes, and Quezon Rep. Danilo Suarez, who garnered 7 votes.

The minority bloc in the Senate has been reduced to just three – Senators Francis Escudero, Antonio Trillanes IV, and Ralph Recto. In the Lower House, the minority bloc would consist of less than 20 congressmen.

Winning is like a magnet. As soon as it became obvious that Duterte would become the next president, congressmen from all parties gravitated towards the victorious party and either defected or agreed to join a coalition that virtually ensured that legislative power would also emanate from the Chief Executive in Malacanang.

And that's where the problem lies. With Duterte assured of control over a co-equal branch, the system of check-and-balance among the three branches of government –executive, legislative and judiciary – has been heavily tilted in favor of the executive branch.

This apparent collusion between the President and the lawmakers becomes even more worrisome because of issues that have been elevated by the ascension of Duterte to the presidency.

For example, the extrajudicial killing of suspected drug dealers has raised concerns about violations of human rights, the deprivation of due process, and failure of the rule of law.

Ordinarily, the recent spate of killings without due process would have set off alarms in the halls of Congress and a congressional probe would have been in order. But the voice of the lone opposition, led by neophyte Senator Leila de Lima, has been drowned by the disturbing silence of the overwhelming majority of Duterte's new allies in both chambers.

Duterte warned Congress during the campaign that if he became president it should not block his efforts to effect change in the government or he would abolish it and form a revolutionary government. Has the usually courageous senators and congressmen, who conducted congressional probes at the drop of a hat, suddenly been cowed by this threat? Or are they afraid they would lose chairmanships of vital congressional committees and the opportunity to include their pet projects during budget deliberations, a cloaked resurrection of the pork barrel?

The check-and-balance mechanism among the co-equal executive, legislative and judiciary branches is one of the most important components of democracy, and ensures that the occupant of Malacanang would not abuse his power. The absolute control of the President over Congress, ensured by the miniscule group of opposition lawmakers, is a surefire invitation to absolute power and eventually tyranny.

It becomes imperative for the Supreme Court to now stand its ground and uphold what is right and just. Its recent decision temporarily stopping curfew ordinances in Manila, Quezon City and Navotas, which is part of Duterte's campaign against criminality, is hopefully an indication that it is ready to uphold the law.

The need for a strong and legitimate opposition becomes even more imperative now that the President is pushing for a constitutional convention to amend the constitution, particularly in converting our form of government into a federal and parliamentary system.

These are issues that need to be thoroughly debated in public and in Congress because they could alter the course of our country. But without a strong critical opposition in Congress, these measures could sail through Congress easily. And with the overwhelming popularity of Duterte, the people could be easily swayed into blindly accepting his actions and proposals.

It is now up to the media and the so-called civil society to provide the critical opposition that would be sorely lacking from the lawmakers and the politicians. A healthy public debate and discourse would ensure that the Duterte administration stays within the law and that any change to the Constitution would be in the best interest of the country.

Ooooo

12
Let's hope change is for real this time
July 26, 2016

WHEN Presidential Communications Secretary Martin Andanar said the first State-of-the-Nation Address (SONA) of President Rodrigo Duterte would be "heart wrenching" and would "make you cry," I just couldn't believe it. It's just not Duterte's style to turn people emotional.

"I don't want to exaggerate. But the first time I read the speech, it made me cry. That's how beautiful and heart-wrenching the President's speech is," Andanar said.

But one and a half hours after Duterte's first words, there were no tears, only laughter, applause and cheers. Duterte supposedly wrote the speech himself and it was estimated to last only 38 minutes – much like his inaugural address – but having veered away from his draft several times to explain in detail the points he had raised, it lasted more than 90 minutes.

There was no complaint, though, because it was the typical Duterte that appeared on that rostrum – no drama, no frills, no slogans, just plain and straightforward pledge to confront the country's many ills in a sustained and relentless manner.

All said in simple Dutertesque manner, in words the ordinary people could understand and relate to.

There was no drama. When Gloria Macapagal Arroyo delivered her first SONA in 2011, she had to use props in the person of three little boys from Payatas and an incredible tale of three paper boats containing the wishes of the poor boys that found its way in Malacanang. Nine years later, the three boys' families remained poor and so did millions of other Filipinos.

Duterte went straight to what he intends to do in almost minute details to solve the country's problems — from fighting the Abu Sayyaf, unclogging the traffic mess, climate change, sustaining the fight against drugs, lowering income taxes, declaring a unilateral ceasefire with the National Democratic Front, ensuring that the reproductive health law would be implemented in its entirety, improving the state of agriculture in the country, pushing for the shift to a federal form of government, the dispute with China, peace in Mindanao, infrastructure, transport woes, OFW welfare, women's rights, the squatter problem, and media killings.

There was no blaming. When Benigno Simeon Aquino III delivered his first SONA in 2010, he spent most of his speech blaming the Arroyo administration for all the ills that his government would have to undo. He spent precious minutes enumerating the faults of his predecessor while disclosing in very general terms how he would solve them.

There was no vindictiveness. Aquino promised to punish people he presumed to be corrupt and did just that a few months later, impeaching and destroying Chief Justice Renato Corona for simple omissions in his Statement of Assets, Liabilities and Net Worth, and jailing Arroyo for six years without trial.

"I will not waste precious time dwelling on the sins of the past or blaming those who are perceived to be responsible for the mess that we are in and suffering from except maybe extract a lesson or two from its errors. We will not tarry because it is the present that we are concerned with and the future that we are concerned for," Duterte said. "Vindictiveness is not in my system."

But he made it clear that those who violated the law shall be brought to justice: "Let me say clearly that those who betray the people's trust shall not go unpunished and they will have their day in court."

There was no sloganeering. Aquino vowed to eliminate poverty and stimulate economic growth by curbing corruption and lead the country from the crooked path to the straight path or "daang matuwid." But it became clear a few years later that the "daang matuwid" was just another slogan, the same as his "kung walang corrupt, walang mahirap" mantra.

There was reassurance. Where before he said that the Abu Sayyafs were not criminals, this time Duterte said, "The full force of the AFP will be applied to crush these criminals who operate under the guise of religious fervor."

On climate change, he said: "Addressing global warming shall be our top priority but upon a fair and equitable equation. It must not stymie our industrialization."

On human rights: "My administration shall be sensitive to the State's obligation to promote and protect, fulfill the human rights of our citizens, especially the poor, the marginalized and the vulnerable."

To mining and logging firms: "Follow government standards. Do not destroy the environment. Follow it to a tee."

On red tape: "We shall enhance local business environment by addressing bottlenecks in business registration and processing, streamlining investment application process and integration the services of various government offices."

On the separation of church and state: "To our religious bishops, leaders, priests, pastors, preachers, imam, let me assure you that while I'm a stickler for the principle of separation between Church and State, I believe quite strongly that there should never be a separation between God and State."

On taxes: "We will lower personal and corporate income tax rates and relax the bank secrecy laws."

With his approval ratings in the low 90s, perhaps the highest in years for a new president, Duterte will have the full support of the people.

Even the usually critical Congress has paved the way for full cooperation, with Duterte's ruling coalition growing beyond expectations as senators and congressmen from parties that were expected to provide the critical opposition joined the victors' bandwagon.

For Duterte and his Cabinet, the hard work begins to make the goals that he has enumerated in Monday's SONA a reality. A year from now, we will either wake up to find that our dreams are beginning to be fulfilled and look forward to even better dreams, or wake up to find we've been had again and another nightmare has begun.

Ooooo

13
Climate change: No excuse for inaction
July 24, 2016

I CANNOT see the logic or the wisdom of President Duterte's statement early this week that the country would not honor the Paris agreement on climate change because it is unfair that developed nations who caused much of the current level of global warming would now want developing countries like the Philippines to contain their carbon emissions to certain levels.

For this reason, he described the historic accord, signed by senior officials of the 195 countries that attended the 21st Conference of Parties in Paris in December last year, as "stupid" and "absurd."

In a sendoff event for a Philippine sports contingent, Duterte, who has a habit of narrating conversations with foreign officials, said he "wanted to kick " an unnamed ambassador when the latter asked him if the Philippines could maintain its carbon emissions.

"I said, 'No. I cannot tell… You don't do it that way, Mr. Ambassador. (Your country) had reached the apex (of industrialization) and along the way put a lot of contaminants and emission and went ahead in destroying the climate,'" the President said.

"We have not reached the age of industrialization. We're now going into it. But you are trying to stymie (our growth) with an agreement that says you can only go up to here," he continued. "That's stupid. I will not honor that."

He added that when the ambassador told him that the Philippines was a signatory to the agreement, Duterte said he replied: "That was not my signature. It's not mine."

Duterte was obviously following the argument of China prior to the Paris meeting that western economies had gained the benefits of carbon-emitting industrialization for decades and now want developing countries to limit carbon emissions and limit their growth.

Even arrogant China saw the danger of continued global warming caused by uncontrolled carbon emissions and joined the other 194 countries in signing the agreement. So far, Chinese President Xi Jin-ping has not declared that he would not honor the Paris agreement because it was not his signature that was on the accord.

By saying that he may not honor the Paris climate change agreement because that he was not the one who signed it, Duterte is opening the door for Xi to also say that he is not obliged to honor the adverse decision of the Permanent Court of Arbitration on the territorial dispute over some areas of the South China Sea because he was not the one who signed the United Nations Convention on the Law of the Sea (Unclos).

This line of reasoning of Duterte, by the way, also runs counter to his declaration shortly before and after his inauguration that he would honor all contracts and commitments entered into by the previous administration. Does this declaration remain valid then? Or will there be more flip flops and inconsistencies down the road?

Of course, I understand where the President is coming from. I'm sure he is sincere in his desire to push the country's economy through industrialization and by doing so, improve the economic wellbeing of our countrymen.

But, as one prominent climate change scientist said, there must be another way to promote industrialization while at the same time trying to protect the environment.

Marine expert Dr. Angel C. Alcala, who is chair of the Silliman University Angelo King Center for Research and Environmental Management, said, "Whether or not we are a non-polluter—because we don't produce as much carbon dioxide as the industrialized nations—we should be in unity with other countries by showing a good example on a globally important environmental issue. Industrialization can continue as planned if there are provisions for sequestering the carbon dioxide produced through activities like planting more areas with forest trees, and protecting our existing tropical rainforests."

Ian Rivera, coordinator of the Philippine Movement for Climate Justice, agreed with Duterte that rich countries are to blame for the current level of global warming. "However, it is difficult now to do away with this global consensus. It will mean going back to several decades of climate negotiations with very little time left before climate catastrophe," he said.

The agreement binds signatory nations to cutting down carbon emissions to contain global warming below 2 degrees Celsius, past which temperature rises would be irreversible. It is disconcerting that the new President does not appear to be concerned about the dangers of global warming considering that the Philippines is one of the most adversely affected by climate change.

In the last few years, the country has been ravaged by super typhoons that have wiped out entire towns, killed thousands, rendered tens of thousands homeless and caused billions of pesos in damages. Scientists have pointed to the warming of the Pacific Ocean as the reason for the stronger and more frequent typhoons in the area.

Years ago, the rainy season in the Philippines traditionally ended in early September, but now typhoons and monsoon rains come almost year-round. Even Mindanao, which before was rarely affected by typhoons, is now experiencing heavy rains and flooding most of the year.

Almost everybody who were affected by these recent weather disturbances all over the world are one in saying they have not experienced such storms and blizzards in years, and yet many are unable to relate these to global warming.

In March 2009, the world's foremost experts on global warming gathered in an emergency meeting in Copenhagen to warn politicians to act now to minimize the impact of what they described could be 'irreversible' climate shifts and hopefully save a world that they said was "on the brink."

The scientists were concerned that any significant delay in reducing emissions would lead to "a range of tipping points" that would make it significantly more difficult to reduce greenhouse gas levels.

The scientists pointed to an increasing possibility that there would be increases in average temperatures of six degrees by the end of the century, which, they said, would produce conditions not seen on Earth for more than 30 million years. That could mean, they added, massive rises in sea level, whole areas devastated by hurricanes and other areas turned into uninhabitable desert, forcing billions of people to leave their homelands.

The 2,500 scientists from 80 countries who attended the conference warned in their statement: "There is no excuse for inaction."

Maybe they should tell that to President Duterte.

Ooooo

14
Change much needed in bureaucracy
July 22, 2016

IF YOU have tried getting a permit, birth certificate or any document from the local government or making any kind of transaction with any government agency in the Philippines, you'd understand why President Duterte warned the country's bureaucrats to be back from lunch at exactly one o'clock.

Duterte said government employees are paid to work eight hours a day, and by extending their lunch breaks with detours to places like shopping malls and casinos, they are "swindling" the people and are, therefore, technically guilty of estafa.

Duterte said he did not want taxpayers being made to go back repeatedly to government offices to secure permits or documents. Those who plan to obtain government documents should be informed beforehand about the necessary requirements and advised on the pickup date.

The government office should also keep a logbook of requests so the employees in charge could estimate the date when the documents would be ready, he said.

Just as he has shown in the drive against illegal drugs, the President appears serious in his warning. Citing a recent letter to the editor of a newspaper where the writer complained about being given the runaround in a government office, he said he would call the particular employee and his chief to explain why they should not be dismissed from government service.

The President has every reason to be angry.

Philippine government employees are perhaps the most spoiled and most unproductive workers in the world. Here's a typical day for most government employees working the 8 a.m. to 5 p.m. shift. He or she will arrive late, around 9 a.m., citing heavy traffic or whatever excuse. They will engage in small talk or spend several minutes in the powder room before finally sit down for work at around 9:30 a.m.

At around 10 a.m., they'll go for a coffee break and come back at least 30 minutes later. At 12 noon, they all leave for lunch outside and as Duterte said, would detour to the shopping mall or even casinos and beer houses. Some would come back at around 2 p.m. and take another break for coffee and merienda around 3 p.m.

At 4:30 p.m., they prepare to leave, packing their bags, powdering their nose and engaging again in small talks. At the strike of exactly 5 p.m., most of them would be gone.

For those not involved in transacting business with people, nobody but themselves and their supervisors would notice what the President calls "swindling." But for those manning counters and dealing with people wishing to obtain documents or filing for applications or benefits, the "swindling" becomes obvious.

People line up as soon as the building's doors open, fall in line for hours and when they finally reach the employees concerned, some are told their papers are not in order and they need to come back the next day, or told it's lunch break and come back at 2 p.m. At 4 p.m., some counters close and the poor taxpayers are told to come back the next day.

It's not just red tape and corruption that have given the government a bad name, and the movement of applications, documents, permits and other transactions crawling in snail's pace. It is also the attitude of many government workers not to take their jobs seriously and to provide the service expected of them as public servants. It is also the arrogant attitude to think that they are doing the people favor when they do their job.

Just as important as going after drug lords and criminals is going after the corrupt, indifferent and unproductive bureaucrats in the government.

Duterte acknowledged that he was elected to the presidency because people are hungry for genuine and meaningful change. "But the change," he stressed during his brief but effective inaugural speech, "if it is to be permanent and significant, should start with us and in us." He added, "We must have the courage and the will to change ourselves."

The change can come in many small ways – lining up for a ride, obeying traffic rules, refusing to bribe policemen and other law enforcers, being courteous to people, and for government workers, reporting on time and doing their work as public servants to the best of their ability.

The change in government, in particular, should come from all levels of government – from the lowly janitor to the highest-ranking officials. Indeed, it will take a lot of courage and the will to effect that change.

Ooooo

15
Sea row: Conflict or cooperation?
July 19, 2016

LAST Tuesday, the Permanent Court of Arbitration in the Netherlands overwhelmingly ruled in favor of the Philippines against China in their territorial dispute over portions of the South China Sea. In unequivocal terms, the UN tribunal ruled that the Philippines has sovereign rights over that part it calls the West Philippine Sea.

In summary, the court, which settles disputes involving the United Nations Convention on the Laws of the Sea (Unclos), ruled in favor of the Philippines over all major points raised by the Philippines, to wit:

• The nine-dash line map being used by China to claim virtually the entire South China Sea was declared invalid and incompatible with Unclos, a treaty ratified by 167 states, including China and the Philippines;

• China's accession to the Unclos means it accepted the limited zones of maritime entitlements in the convention, hence, China cannot assert its theory of historic rights to living and non-living resources in the West Philippine Sea;

• China's law enforcement activities in the area were declared illegal;

• China's land reclamation and island creation activities were declared illegal; and

• Geographic features do not generate maritime zone entitlements that support China's claims to 89 percent of the sea.

In a perfect world, the Philippines can now focus on securing the islands and the waters in the area and tapping it for economic gains for the country and its people. Fishermen can again fish the fertile waters of the sea, Philippine consortiums can start digging for oil and natural gas, and commercial vessels can freely pass over its waters.

But ours is an imperfect world, made even more so by rogue leaders who wish to impose their will on other people and smaller nations.

China, which from the start has refused to participate in the proceedings nor accept any ruling that the tribunal would make despite being a signatory to Unclos, steadfastly reject the decision, saying the ruling was null and void and that Beijing would not accept it.

President Xi Jinping of China insisted that the South China Sea has been Chinese territory since "ancient times" and said China's territorial sovereignty and interests in the region would not be influenced under any circumstances by the ruling.

"This farce is now over," said Foreign Minister Wang Yi. "China opposes and will never accept any claim or action based on those awards."

The ministry stressed that the Philippines' move to initiate arbitration without China's consent had been in "bad faith" and in violation of international law. These are arrogant words from a nation that has been declared in violation of international law (Unclos) by encroaching on the Philippines' exclusive economic zone (EEZ) and by refusing to accept a ruling by a tribunal created by international law.

The United States, the European Union and other western powers, which have stressed the need to maintain freedom of navigation in the area and the rule of law, cautioned China against rejecting the verdict and warned both sides to avoid provocative statements and actions that would only intensify the conflict.

China, for its part, cautioned of conflict and confrontations and warned western powers against turning the South China Sea into a "cradle of war." Beijing threatened to establish an air defense zone there, after its claims to the strategically vital waters were declared invalid.

A Chinese military expert said China might choose to take a hard line with the Philippines, perhaps taking punitive measures such as sanctions, to send a message to other claimants, such as Vietnam, Malaysia and Indonesia to adopt a prudent attitude on the South China Sea issue.

While blaming the Philippines for "stirring trouble" in the South China Sea by relying on "distorted facts and concocted a pack of lies" to push forward the arbitration proceedings, Beijing remains optimistic about bilateral negotiations with Manila.

"China stands ready to work with the new Philippine government," Chinese Vice Foreign Minister Liu Zhenmin said, adding that "early removal of obstacles posed by the arbitration case" would help improve relations.

The biggest question now is what will the Philippine government do next? Despite the overwhelming victory in the sea claims case, the Duterte administration continues to send mixed signals.

Presidential spokesman Ernesto Abella said the administration is preparing, in consultation with experts, the "right response at the right time, " adding that the Philippines welcomes the arbitration court's decision, but will proceed with "sobriety and restraint."

The call for sobriety and restraint seems the correct move at this time, knowing fully well that the new administration has not really made a definitive stand on the issue although President Duterte and Foreign Affairs Secretary Perfecto Yasay Jr. have both said the country is willing to go into bilateral talks with China.

But by constantly saying that the Philippines is leaning towards holding bilateral talks, the government is dissipating the advantage it has gained through the victory in the tribunal.

China expert Chito Sta. Romana, who lived and worked in China for more than three decades from the time he was struck in Beijing with two other Filipino college students upon the declaration of martial law in 1972 and was Beijing bureau chief for ABC, said in a speech before the Makati Business Club that the Philippines should proceed with caution and restraint, but without fear. That was said nearly a year before the tribunal ruling.

"The key is to seek a peaceful, diplomatic solution that will be mutually beneficial; in other words, a win-win formula. Brinkmanship can only lead to a dead-end, if not a disaster… But the basic approach should be to engage China while at the same time hedging our bets and preparing for any eventuality. That is, a combination of engagement and hedging," Sta. Romana said. By hedging and preparing for any eventuality means to build a minimum credible defense and to line up support from the U.S. and other allies and friends, he added.

The question remains, even after the favorable tribunal ruling and pledge of support from Western powers, whether the Duterte administration would choose cooperation over conflict. Which one would it be?

Ooooo

16
All people's lives matter
July 13, 2016

MORE THAN a century and a half after the a bloody civil war ended slavery in the United

States, and almost half a century after the civil rights movement ended decades of segregation and discrimination, the nation is again teetering back to the dark ages of racism following the bloody developments of the past week.

The shooting to death of two black men by police officers in Louisiana and Minnesota early in the week triggered nationwide protests against indiscriminate killing of unarmed blacks by the police. The peaceful protests were usurped by the senseless shooting of 12 Dallas police officers, five of them ending up dead, by a lone black gunman, who was himself killed during a standoff with responding policemen.

It was a chaotic close to a bloody week, a carnage that has brought America back on the edge of a racial crisis. A day after, people from all sides of the racial divide were back on the streets nationwide to grieve, to protest and to vent their anger over what is happening to this country.

The two top police officials of Dallas echoed what many of those protesters were saying.

"This must stop, this divisiveness between our police and our citizens," said Dallas's police chief, David Brown, who is black.

"We have devolved into some separatism and we've taken our corners," Malik Aziz, the deputy chief of police, told CNN. "Days like yesterday or the day before, they shouldn't happen. But when they do, let's be human beings. Let's be honorable men and women and sit down at a table and say, 'How can we not let this happen again?' and be sincere in our hearts. We're failing at that on all sides."

The police official was talking about the shooting of the police officers and the shooting to death of two black men the day before in Louisiana and Minnesota.

The police shootings in Louisiana and Minnesota – the 122nd and 123rd killing of a black man by police officers so far this year, according to the American Civil Liberties Union – were both caught in videos that shocked the already angry and scared American people, particularly those in the African-American community.

The first video showed Alton Sterling pinned to the ground outside a store in Baton Rouge, Louisiana, when he was shot in the chest and back at close range by police officers.

The second video showed the death of Philando Castile, who was shot several times by a police officer after he was stopped for an alleged traffic infraction in a St. Paul suburb in Minnesota. The video, which was taken by his girlfriend, Diamond Reynolds, who was sitting next to him in the car, starts seconds after Castile was shot. "He was just getting his license and registration, sir," the girlfriend calmly tells the officer. She says to the camera that he was not reaching for the gun he was licensed to carry.

"Would this have happened if the passengers, the drivers were white? I don't think it would have," Gov. Mark Dayton said at a news conference on Thursday. "All of us in Minnesota are forced to confront that this kind of racism exists."

This is the same question people have been asking since the issue of indiscriminate police shooting of black people came to national attention with the 2014 killing of Michael Brown, an unarmed black teenager, in an encounter with a white officer in Ferguson, Missouri.

The Ferguson shooting triggered protests in Ferguson and elsewhere for nearly a year and a half before the city government agreed to reforms after Department of Justice investigators found that police officers there regularly violated constitutional rights. The report said minority citizens were routinely harassed by police officers and shuttled through a court system that further exploited and victimized local residents.

But the police shootings did not stop in Ferguson. In Chicago, for example, 17-year-old Laquan McDonald was shot 16 times also in 2014 by a police officer later indicted on charges of first-degree murder. And obviously there were scores more such incidents as revealed by ACLU.

But even more frightening is what has transpired after last week's killings. It would seem that the anger that black people have been keeping in their hearts has begun to explode with the ambush of the Dallas police officers, who were there to help secure the protesters and to keep the rally peaceful. Another ominous sign is the reported presence of some alleged members of the Black Panthers who were seen carrying shotguns. Under Texas laws, people are allowed to carry licensed gun in public.

Even more frightening is the reaction of many white supremacists as shown in social media where many of them are calling on fellow neo-Nazis to take up arms and be prepared for a "racial war."

Some print and online publications are not helping any to mitigate the anger between the two sides of the racial divide, and are in fact pouring gas into the flames. The New York Post, for example, splashed the inflammatory headline 'CIVIL WAR" on its front page after the Dallas shooting while The Drudge Report, an ultra-conservative news website, bannered "BLACK LIVES KILL" on its first page.

The violence of the past week should not result in further violence. They should instead prod local officials to institute reforms to make police officers more respectful of the citizens they have been tasked to protect.

Black Lives Matter. That's the movement that came to life after the Ferguson shooting. Law enforcement officer should start looking at black people and other minority persons not as criminals, but as human beings because people's lives matter.

The violence – from both sides of the racial divide – should stop. Let not America go back to the dark ages of racism. As Attorney General Loretta Lynch pleaded after the Dallas carnage: "Turn to each other, not against each other.

Ooooo

17
Hopefully, relief from hunger

July 13, 2016

FOR DECADES, Filipino politicians have courted the poor in their campaigns, and for good reason, of course, the poor having the most number of votes and being the most gullible among the nation's voting groups. Most of those who associated themselves with the poor or who claimed to champion their cause have won election to important posts in both the House and the Senate and to the presidency.

It is ironic that while the poor have been responsible for the election of nearly all of these politicians, their economic situation has worsened through the years. In fact, their numbers have grown through the years that they elected alleged "champions of the poor" who promised to uplift them from their poverty and relieve them from hunger.

In 2010, then Sen. Benigno S. Aquino III rode on the crest of the popularity of his recently demised mother and on his promise to eliminate poverty by curbing corruption, as exemplified by his mantra "kung walang corrupt, walang mahirap," to win the presidential elections overwhelmingly.

Six years later, the poor has remained poor and the hungry even hungrier.

A survey by the Social Weather Stations, conducted on the waning days of the Aquino administration from March 30 to April 2, showed that more Filipinos experienced involuntary hunger at least once in the preceding three months, with their numbers growing to 3.1 million families from the 2.6 million families in the December survey, and bringing the hunger rate to 13.7 percent of the population, up from 11.7 percent.

Of the 3.1 million families, some 2.6 million said they experienced "moderate hunger" (going hungry only once or a few times in the last three months) while some 481,000 families said they suffered "severe hunger" ("often" or "always" hungry in the last three months).

The survey results run counter to claims by the Aquino administration that it has cut back poverty by curbing corruption and that it has helped millions of poor families put food on the table with its Conditional Cash Transfer plan, a social amelioration program.

In the beginning of his term, Aquino repeatedly boasted that the country will no longer have to import rice for the people's daily needs by 2013 and would, in fact, be a rice exporting nation by 2014.

And yet as of end of that year, the country imported more than 705,000 metric tons of rice and the price of the staple continued to rise. The funny thing is that despite the obvious disparity between supply and demand, the government shifted its focus from attaining rice self-sufficiency to the farming of alternative, high-value crops such as pineapple, bananas and dragon fruit, among others.

While producing high-value crops is good for exports, the country needs to continue attaining self-sufficiency in rice for the simple reason that it is the basic staple of Filipinos. By encouraging the shift to high-value crops, most of the rice farmers would abandon rice planting, resulting in a potential food crisis that the government would find difficult to handle.

The policy shift was a capitulation by the government to capitalists, who are more interested in the profits that high-value crops could bring to them, rather than in the needs of the millions of Filipinos who are dependent on rice and vegetables. While the export of these high-value crops would enrich them, it would spell more difficulties for the impoverished people who will have to contend with much higher prices of rice and vegetables, and for farmers who stand to lose their livelihoods.

"Don't obey. Don't listen to the dictate of a landlord president," Kilusang Magbubukid ng Pilipinas national president Rafael Mariano, who is now the Duterte administration's agrarian reform secretary, told the movement's over 1.3 million members in 65 provincial chapters and 15 regional chapters nationwide following the announcement of the policy shift.

The results of the failure of the Aquino administration's agriculture program despite billions of dollars allotted for feeds, fertilizers, irrigation and other support programs that only went to the pockets of dirty politicians and greedy businessmen and its intentional delaying of the full implementation of the Comprehensive Agrarian Reform Program (CARP) can now be clearly seen with more Filipinos hungry as shown by surveys after surveys.

President Duterte made it very clear that food sufficiency and lower food prices, particularly on rice, is his administration's priority fghgfghfwhen he appointed a farmer, former North Cotabato Governor Manny Pinol, to the agriculture department. "My task is to make sure that there will be enough food for Filipinos and improve the lives of our farmers," said Pinol, who was among the first to be named to the Duterte Cabinet.

Mariano is also a farmer and was the first genuine farmer to serve as a member of the House of Representatives in 2004. The president of Kilusang Magbubukid ng Pilipinas and national president of the party-list Anakpawis, Mariano's appointment to the Department of Agrarian Reform was hailed by farmers and sent shivers to the country's landlords.

Now that true farmers are at the helm of the two lead agencies involved in food production, it is hoped that the millions of poor Filipinos will finally find relief from hunger, and not just promised deliverance by uncaring politicians. We shall find out soon enough.

Ooooo

18
Honoring the sanctity of contracts
July 9, 2016

AMONG the very first directives of President Rodrigo Duterte to his Cabinet during its first meeting shortly after his inauguration was to honor government contracts and to implement measures to further ease doing business in the country. These measures bode well for the government's efforts to attract more investments into the country and accelerate economic development.

While it is true that the Philippine economy registered satisfactory growth during the administration of President Benigno S. Aquino III, it can also be argued that the growth could have been higher had the government not slowed down infrastructure development when it suspended or rescinded several contracts that were reached during the time of his predecessor, Gloria Macapagal Arroyo.

Aquino, who blamed Arroyo for just about anything that didn't go well during his administration, was so paranoid that he ordered nearly all contracts signed during the Arroyo administration, including major infrastructure projects, reviewed, suspended or rescinded.

This brought the country in a bad light among foreign investors and even local businessmen. It also slowed down and deterred foreign investments, and consequently the growth of the economy.

Among the earliest contracts that Aquino ordered cancelled was the one with the Belgian firm Baggerwerken Decloedt En Zoon (BDZ) to dredge the Laguna de Bay for P18 billion.

Aquino canceled the dredging project, which aims to prevent water levels from rising and causing floods in nearby areas, after learning of allegedly questionable components of the project. He said the project was "illogical" since the dredged material would simply be dumped into another part of the lake.

"Even a Grade 5 student will easily see that this project is illogical," he said. "There are still people who think they can pull a fast one that would cost at least P18.5 billion," Aquino said.

But the Kilusang Lawa Kalikasan, an environmental group, said the President may have been misinformed about the project.

Obviously, whoever advised Aquino to cancel the project based his conclusion on a Grade 5 student's logic. The project was the result of years of research, study and evaluation by a team of experts whose findings and recommendations were reviewed by the National Economic Development Authority (NEDA) and experts from the Belgian government, which was going to provide the funding through its overseas development assistance (ODA) program.

The Belgian government was reportedly so incensed by Malacanang's unilateral scrapping of the contract and the "unprofessional" and "improper" act of announcing it to the press without informing the other party first that it threatened to hold all ODA funding to the Philippines in abeyance.

The European Chamber of commerce of the Philippines (ECCP) in December cited other contracts affected by changes of policies midstream, particularly the deal between the Philippine International Air Terminal Co. (Piatco) and German airport contractor Fraport AG and the government for the construction of Naia Terminal 3.

ECCP Vice President Henry Schumacher said Terminal 3 is now widely used, but the contractor has not been paid despite a decision by an arbitration court.

ECCP also cited the case of the water contracts issue between MWSS and water concessionaires Manila Water Company Inc. and Maynilad Water Services Inc., where a dispute over rates later came about despite specific provisions on water charges in the contract with the government.

ECCP officials said contracts not being honored must be based on "concrete proof" that the agreements are onerous and not on mere allegations of wrongdoing. The ECCP also cited the dispute on the license-plate standardization project of the Land Transportation Office (LTO). The Department of Transportation and Communications signed a five-year contract with JKG-Power Plates, a joint venture between a Dutch firm and a Filipino company after conducting a bidding process in 2014 for the supply of vehicle license plates worth P3.18 billion.

On the basis of this signed contract, JKG-Power Plates delivered 877,166 pairs of MV plates, 2,370,006 MC plates, and 12,685 trailer plates worth P620.35 million. However, they have only been paid P477.90 million.

Another prominent case cited by businessmen was the cancellation by the DOTC of a contract with a reputable firm to maintain and operate the Metro Rail Transit 3 (MRT 3). The DOTC gave the project to what columnist Peter Wallace described as "an unknown, untested newcomer for supposedly potential cash savings that would now actually entail a huge cost."

Wallace also cited a critically important project, an air navigation system, that he said was held up for 21 months for no valid reason.

There's also the Poverty Eradication and Alleviation Certificates, or PEACe bonds, in which the Bureau of Internal Revenue (BIR) reneged on its promise that the bonds would be treated as tax-free, Wallace said.

"All these cases present a very negative image of this government—one that doesn't keep its word, one that doesn't honor contracts, and one that doesn't obey court orders," Wallace pointed out.

With the assurance from the Duterte administration that it would honor all government contracts entered into by the previous administration, business leaders are heaving a sigh of relief.

Duterte ordered all department secretaries and heads of agencies to remove redundant requirements and that compliance with one department or agency, shall be accepted as sufficient for all. He also ordered them to "refrain from changing and bending rules, government contracts, transactions and projects already approved and awaiting implementation".

It seems all the fears that business leaders and other sectors expressed shortly after Duterte's victory had been erased in the new President's very first day. Let us hope that the rough ride that Duterte wants us all to join with him would be worth taking after all.

Ooooo

19
A different, better Duterte
July 3, 2016

THE Filipino people met a different Rodrigo Duterte on his first day in Malacanang. No curses, no threats, none of those checkered Duterte shirts. Instead, he was described as "presidential, purposeful and persuasive" during his 15-minute inaugural speech following his swearing in as the 16th president of the Republic of the Philippines in Malacanang. And he was wearing a barong Tagalog with a Philippine flag pinned on his lapel, not the usual jean and shirt attire as many had expected.

His speech, described by Ateneo School of Government Dean Antonio La Vina as one of the best speeches he has ever heard, was "good, plain, straight to the point, consistent with his advocacies, but this time there is reassurance about knowing his limits."

A look at the reactions of senators, congressmen and even the usually critical newspapers points to a very good start by the usually tough-talking former Davao mayor in his six-year presidency.

Sen. Ralph Recto described the speech best: "Like a great woman's dress, it was long enough to cover the subject, but short enough to be interesting. It proved that brevity need not be junked to accommodate a host of bold statements."

Recto said he believed the address covered the breadth of things Duterte initially wanted to do, balancing audacity with guarantees that his administration wouldn't go overboard in pursuing them.
"He will go hard after criminals but not at the expense of killing the rule of law. He will comfort the afflicted but not by impoverishing the already comfortable. He will help laborers but will not harm capital in the process," Recto said.

He noted that Duterte's pronouncements struck the right mix of being bold but responsible. He said they were courageous and comforting at the same time.

Sen. Loren Legarda hasd this to say: "We can see the sincerity in the President's words, the single-mindedness of a true leader, the political will to bring a government that truly serves the people with passion, vision, and compassion. I am very optimistic that we can fully push for inclusive, equitable, and sustainable growth under the new administration as the President himself embraces these concepts and reaches out to all sectors of society."

"The speech was direct to the point. President Duterte's speech is a glimpse of what we should expect from his administration: straightforward, unembellished [and] unpretentious," said Rep. Karlo Alexei Nograles of Davao City.

"For the first time, he did not mouth curses. He promised that as soon as he assumed power, he would no longer throw invectives. And he did not," said Ramon Casiple, executive director of Institute for Political and Electoral Reform (IPER).

The Philippine Daily Inquirer, a usually critical newspaper, said Duterte's presidency is off to a very good start, with "a powerfully argued inaugural address that set forth his vision of governance in clear, compelling terms."

The Inquirer said Duterte delivered a "carefully written, well-calibrated speech—and yet it did not for a moment sound inauthentic. It was the real Duterte, the veteran prosecutor who was equally at home in English and the language of the law, the successful local executive who proudly points to both his law and order record and his city's thriving example, the long-time politician who has thought often about the country's biggest problems."

The Manila Standard, another tough-talking newspaper, was all praises: "President Rodrigo Duterte's inaugural speech was a stark departure from his previous statements and his demeanor in the past few weeks. It was a good first day in office.

"Those who were anticipating a strongly worded speech from the usually tough-talking Duterte were surprised that he was presidential— calm and even tentative in a few unguarded moments, as if he were just coming to terms with the overwhelming task that lay before him."

After winning the hearts of more than 16 million Filipinos, it is obvious that Duterte has persuaded a few more millions to believe in him, or at least to give him a chance to prove his worth as the nation's leader.

He appeared sincere when he said the road ahead would be rough. "The ride will be rough but come and join me just the same. Together, shoulder to shoulder, let us take the first wobbly steps in this quest," he said.

To show he meant business in his quest for real change, Duterte set the tone for his governance right in the very first meeting with his Cabinet, just hours after telling the people the direction of his administration.

He told the Cabinet members to forget special treatment. "I don't want special treatment. There's no stopping of activities just because of somebody," he said. He ordered Transportation Secretary Arthur Tugade to instruct the Civil Aviation Authority of the Philippines to scrap the "no-fly zone" protocol at the airports to accommodate presidential flights.

"I want this stopped," he said. "We should not be treated differently from the other suffering Filipino passengers. It's not good."

His predecessor, President Benigno S. Aquino III said as much when he initiated his "wang wang" policy, but it was forgotten just as soon. We are confident that Duterte would pursue his own no VIP policy throughout his term.

Another first-day incident at Malacanang that was so surreal the Inquirer reporter described it as such was when he invited activists outside Malacanang to come in and dialogued with them. In previous administrations, marchers were stopped on Mendiola Bridge with barbed wires and troops.

Rollie Macasaet, one of the original members of his core group, during his visit to Los Angeles told us that Duterte is a very intelligent and decent man and that when he talks tough and makes jokes during campaign sorties, he was just trying to entertain the crowd and tell them what they wanted to hear. But once he becomes president, he will act like a president.

After Duterte's first day in office, many believe him now.

Ooooo

20

States seize gun control initiative

July 3, 2016

A 15-hour filibuster by Connecticut Sen. Chris Murphy and a daylong sit-in by 170 lawmakers in the Capitol failed to stir Congress into legislative action on gun control, but states are seizing the initiative to institute tougher measures to prevent gun violence.

Murphy, who represented the district that included Newtown while a congressman, ended his filibuster past 2 a.m. happy with the thought that he had convinced some senators to help push a measure to assure that those on the terrorist watch list do not get guns and an amendment to expand background checks on gun shows and on internet gun sales.

The House Democrats, led by Reps. John Lewis and Nancy Pelosi, took over the House floor literally, not even giving way to security and maintenance personnel, to press for votes to expand background checks and ban gun sales to those on the no-fly watch list.

The Democrats in the Senate and in the House vowed to continue their fight for tighter gun control in the wake of a series of mass shootings, including the Orlando massacre where 50 people were killed and 53 more were injured by a gunman who had been under the FBI radar but was still able to purchase an assault rifle and a handgun.

But the Republicans, backed by a strong gun lobby from the National Rifle Association, apparently wouldn't budge, prompting the usual gridlock in Washington. The national debate over gun control has been going on for decades, but nothing has moved forward in the federal level.

With the federal leaders' failure to move to restrict gun ownership or even fund research on gun violence, states are beginning to take the initiative to restrict gun ownership to further avert violence and killings perpetrated by persons who have gained access to high-powered firearms because of lack of background checks.

California, which already has one of the toughest gun ownership restrictions in the country, for example passed legislation to establish a firearm violence research center at the University of California, filling the gap left by Congressional restrictions on firearms research, on June 16, four days after the Orlando massacre, the deadliest mass shooting in American history.

"We in California already have benefitted from many years of research done at the UC Davis School of Medicine Violence Prevention Research Center. We know that using real data and scientific methods, our best researchers can help policy makers get past the politics and find real answers to this public health crisis to help save lives in California and throughout the country," said State Senator Lois Wolk (D-Davis), whose legislation, Senate Bill 1006, was included as part of the state budget agreed to by Gov. Jerry Brown and the State Legislature.

The 2016-2017 state budget now includes $5 million to establish the California Firearm Violence Research Center, to be allocated over a five-year period. The research center will conduct interdisciplinary research to provide the scientific evidence upon which to base sound firearm violence prevention policies and programs. The center will also work with the legislature and state agencies to identify, implement, and evaluate innovative firearm violence prevention policies and programs.

Two weeks earlier, the California State Senate also passed a bill authored by Sen. Richard Pan, who is a medical doctor, and co-authored by Senator Bill Monning, which would allow California to partner at the federal level to reduce gun violence. SB 877 will require California to establish and maintain a data-tracking system on violent deaths in the state, including gun deaths.

"Researchers cannot fully confront the crisis and save lives because we lack research and tracking," said Pan. "As a doctor, I've seen the horrors of gun violence first-hand and central to preventing such violence is data-centered research."

California is not the only state that has moved to avert gun violence after the Orlando shooting.

Hawaii last week enacted a series of gun laws, one of which makes it the first state to put firearm owners into a database.

That database, which is called the "Rap Back" system, is operated by the FBI and would notify police when a gun owner is arrested for a crime anywhere in the United States.

"This will allow county police departments in Hawaii to evaluate whether the firearm owner may continue to legally possess and own firearms," the Hawaii governor's office said in a statement.

The Hawaii Legislature passed a second and separate gun measure Thursday that prohibits offenders who have stalked or committed sexual assault from owning guns. At least 11 other states have some sort of laws restricting people who've been convicted of stalking from possessing guns.

The third new law requires Hawaii gun owners to surrender their firearms and ammunition to the police if they've been disqualified to possess the weapons "due to a diagnosis of having a significant behavioral, emotional, or mental disorder, or due to emergency or involuntary admission to a psychiatric facility." If the person does not voluntarily give up their arms, the police chief has permission to seize the weapons.

More than a dozen other states have strengthened laws over the past two years to keep firearms out of the hands of domestic abusers, a rare area of consensus in the nation's highly polarized debate over guns. Debates are expected this year over similar proposals in several states.

The Center for American Progress report finds that states with stronger laws have fewer gun deaths per capita, while states with weaker laws have more gun deaths. The politicians in Washington, particularly the NRA-backed Republicans, have ignored this finding for decades despite the series of mass killings in the country.

With the political gridlock in Washington stalling moves to avert gun violence, we can relish the fact that states are seizing the initiative on gun control.

Ooooo

21
Like drug dealers, Abus should be eliminated

June 26, 2016

WHILE we agree that eliminating the growing drug problem in the country should be a priority for the incoming administration of Rodrigo Duterte, we also hope that the tough-talking President-elect would give the same importance to removing from the face of the earth the other scourge of humanity, the Abu Sayyaf Group (ASG).

The Abu Sayyaf, which had been quiet the past few years, has resumed its criminal activities in the last few months with the kidnapping of several foreigners. The Islamic separatist group, which has degenerated into a band of bandits after the death of its founder, Abdurajik Abubakar Janjalani, in 1998 and his brother, Khadaffy Janjalani, in 2007, has gained international attention and notoriety following the beheading of two of their captives, Canadians John Risdell and Robert Hall.

The ASG carried out the beheadings after the Canadian government refused to pay ransom of P300 million for each after separate deadlines in the past two months. They are still holding captive Norwegian Kjartan Sekkingstad and the Filipino Maritess Flor, for whom they are also demanding P300 million each. More hostages, both foreign and Filipino, languish in other Abu Sayyaf camps.

Earlier, the Abu Sayyaf had released 10 Indonesia crewmembers of a fishing boat after the shipping company reportedly paid a total of P50 million for their freedom. In the past several years, the group had beheaded other hostages after no ransom was paid and released some after payment of ransom in the millions of pesos.

For as long as foreign governments and companies continue to meet the ransom demands of these bandits, there will be more kidnappings because the Abu Sayyaf at this time exists for the same goal as other criminal groups – money.

The Canadian government rightfully refused to heed the Abu Sayyaf's demand for ransom although it had to pay the price – the violent death of two of its citizens.

"The government of Canada will not and cannot pay ransoms for hostages to terrorist groups, as doing so would endanger the lives of more Canadians," Prime Minister Justin Trudeau said as he called on his colleagues in the G-7, a grouping of the world's richest nations, to stop paying ransom to kidnapers. With ransoms in the millions of pesos paid, the Abu Sayyaf will have enough money to purchase more arms and recruit more fighters to carry out even more abductions.

The bigger danger, however, is that with more funds, more arms and more fighters, the Abu Sayyaf can focus its attention again on its separatist and terrorist goals.

In 2000, the Abu Sayyad had about 1,250 fighters that dwindled to just about 200 to 400 members in 2012. From 2000 to 2014, some 500 people had been killed as a result of the ASG's activities that include bombings, kidnappings, and assassinations.

The Abu Sayyaf, which means "father of the swordsman" or "father of the sword" in Arabic, was responsible for the Philippines' worst terrorist attack in 2004, the bombing of Superferry 14, which killed 116 people.

Originally formed to create an independent Islamic state encompassing Mindanao and parts of Borneo, southern Thailand and the Sulu archipelago, the Abu Sayyaf will be a major threat to Duterte's goal of forging peace with the two other separatist groups – the Moro National Liberation Front (MNLF) and the Moro Islamic Liberation Front (MILF).

Abu Sayyaf was formed on the principle that jihad is the only way to attain real peace, justice and righteousness and that the Koran and sunnah (the traditions of the Prophet Muhammad and his companions) are the sole guiding authorities for a future new society.

While the MNLF and MILF are agreeable to an autonomous state under a federal system of government, the Abu Sayyaf, once it has rebuilt its army of dedicated fighters, would most probably refuse to deviate from its original goal of a fully independent Islamic state ruled by shariah law.

The Abu Sayyaf has recently released a video where the group pledged allegiance to the Islamic State (IS) and this could mean a bigger headache for the incoming Duterte government since IS-affiliated groups are more violent and more prone to committing terrorist acts.

The spate of Abu Sayyaf kidnappings has already put a damper on the emergence of tourism as a major sector in the Philippine economy. Several foreign governments have issued travel warnings to the Philippines, particularly in the southern part of the country, because of the threat poised by the Abu Sayyaf.

The military has deployed 5,000 troops to go after the Abu Sayyaf bandits, but numerical superiority has not given the AFP an advantage as the Abus has better knowledge of the rugged terrain and people living in the three barangays where they reportedly operate are said to be protecting them because the residents are given shares of the bounty from the kidnappings.

There are moves to declare martial law in the area to enable the military to move more freely. President Aquino himself has said that he had entertained the idea of declaring martial law three weeks before the deadline on the payment of ransom for Hall was set to expire to enable the troops to pursue the Abus and save the hostages.

Aquino said he did not declare martial law because he would need to deploy so many forces with no guarantee of positive results. "There might even be negative results. There might be additional sympathy [for] our enemies here," Aquino said.

Richard J. Gordon, who was recently elected to another term in the Senate, agrees that a strong government is needed to solve kidnappings in Mindanao and avoid possible foreign intervention in the country's counter-terrorism campaign.

Even the Commission on Human Rights expressed support for the government's campaign to "apply the full force of the law" against the Abu Sayyaf.

"These despicable acts of the [Abu Sayyaf] have no place in a civilized society," according to the CHR, which said it supported the campaign of the national government to apply the "full force of the law, arrest all perpetrators of these heinous crimes, bring them before the bar of justice, and to ensure accountability."

President Aquino has started unleashing the "full force of the law" but with just a few days left of his term, his hands are obviously tied from staging the war against the Abu Sayyaf more forcefully and is expected to hand over the mission to Duterte.

Will Duterte use the same strong-arm tactics he has vowed to use against the drug dealers and other criminal elements in eliminating this other scourge of society? I think he should, and then show the people in the area that the government has not neglected them by aggressively pursuing the development of the region.

It should not just be a battle of arms and ammos, but for the hearts and minds of the people.

Ooooo

22
Agriculture: Back to the basics
June 26, 2016

UP UNTIL the 70s, Philippine agriculture was the envy of our Asian neighbors. The country was one of the largest producers of rice, coconut, sugar, abaca and corn. The country also boasted of producing the best varieties of rice, including the famous milagrosa. Agriculture students from all over Asia studied in the world-famous International Rice Research Institute in Los Banos, Laguna.

But something happened along the way because today, despite still being primarily an agricultural country, the Philippines lags behind some of its neighbors in terms of production, marketing and technology.

Incoming Agriculture Secretary Manny Pinol, a former newsman and close friend during our days pounding the news desk in Manila, laments that Thailand, Taiwan, Vietnam, and other Asian neighbors have passed the Philippines in generating revenues from agriculture.

Pinol, a farmer himself in his native M'lang, North Cotabato, laid out his plans for Philippine agriculture in a forum hosted by Emma Tiebens of the Filipino-American Chamber of Commerce of Orange Country (FACCOC) Wednesday night in Irvine.

He blamed corruption for the sad state of Philippine agriculture, pointing out that billions of pesos that were allotted to support farmers in terms of seeds, fertilizers, equipment, and farm-to-market roads went to the pockets of greedy politicians and businessmen.

There have been many agricultural programs that were designed to help small farmers, but many of them failed because while the intent of the programs were noble on paper, it soon became clear that the initiators and enforcers did not really have the interest of the farmers in mind, but only their own selfish interests.

One need not look far down history to see that under the kind of leadership that we have had, any agricultural development program was bound to fail.

Under the administration of Gloria Macapagal Arroyo, billions of pesos were allotted to programs that were designed to help the farmers achieve economic independence. Among these were the P720-million fertilizer fund, the P3.1-billion irrigation project, the P5-billion swine program, the P120-M Gintong Masagana Ani (GMA) program, and the P455-million ice-making machine program for fishermen.

For some reason, the release of the funds for all these projects was timed a few months before the elections in 2004, 2007 and 2010.

The fertilizer millions apparently did not go to the farmers but went to the campaign kitties of the administration party's candidates for congressmen, governors and mayors. The P5 billion that were supposed to be used to buy piglets for farmers were also obviously derailed because not a single piglet's shriek was heard. What ever happened to the P3.1 billion for irrigation projects is unknown because I have not heard of a single dam or irrigation canal built under the program. And the P455 million probably froze before any ice could be made from the non-existent ice machines.

Whatever happened to all those programs? Were they ever implemented? How much were released, and how much have been done? Will they ever be implemented?

The politicians must stop using the farmers for their own agenda. The Philippines has been lagging behind its neighbors in agriculture, which propelled many Asian nations, such as Thailand, Indonesia, Taiwan, and Vietnam to rapid economic growth.

The country needs to go back to the basics. Agriculture can provide the answer to spreading economic development to the provinces, which, in turn, will help decongest the urban centers. A successful agrarian reform program, with the government providing full support to the farmer beneficiaries, can help boost countryside development, and consequently, national economic recovery.

But first, corruption must be curbed. President Aquino was right when he said "kung walang corrupt walang mahirap" but didn't do much to cleanse the government of corruption. The Department of Agriculture and the Department of Agrarian Reform are still perceived to be two of the most corrupt agencies under the Aquino administration.

Pinol assures his audience that under the administration of incoming President Rodrigo Duterte, elimination of corruption in all levels of government will be the priority. If the billions of pesos allotted to agriculture in the previous administrations were spent for the purpose for which they were intended, there is no reason the Philippines would lag behind its Asian neighbors in agriculture.

Piñol said his marching order from Duterte was to secure food availability and affordability to Filipinos and stop corruption in the department. He said he has identified three major components to focus on as an immediate intervention to assist farmers: fast and effective agricultural technology-transfer to farmers, easy access to financing, and efficient marketing for farmer's produce. He also said he intends to build small irrigation systems powered by solar energy to provide much needed water to small farms all over the country.

These are all great ideas from a practicing farmer, instead of just a bureaucrat administering from a desk in Manila. But the agriculture department also has to look at how it can lure the youth back to the farms.

The Technical Education and Skills Development Authority (TESDA) reported in 2011 that the average age of the country's farmers has reached around 50 years old. The government should address this situation immediately. There is a need to create a steady pool of farm workers to prevent an acute shortage of agricultural workers in the near future.

The government should increase funding for the various state agricultural colleges in the provinces and offer scholarships to those who profess a passion for agriculture. The country needs to revive the interest of the Filipino youth to get them involved in agriculture.

The Philippines has millions of hectares of arable land and has an abundance of water rich in fish and other marine products, and yet agriculture accounts for only about 12 percent of the country's gross domestic product (GDP), even lower than the share of foreign remittances. Given the proper training and incentives, agriculture can regain its status as the premier revenue-producing sector in the country. Hopefully, Pinol can provide the leadership to achieve that.

Ooooo

23
Sea row: Where does Duterte really stand?
June 12, 2016

WITH the United States and China getting bolder and bolder in their raging word war over the South China Sea, it is becoming increasingly probable that the conflict could come to a head in the near future. And while several countries both in the Asia-Pacific and in Europe have made clear their stand on the issue, it seems the incoming leadership in the Philippines has not made up its mind where to stand in case the crisis escalates further.

President-elect Rodrigo Duterte has sent mixed signals on where he actually stands on the issue. During the campaign and in one of his early press conferences, Duterte said he was ready to enter into bilateral talks with China on their conflicting claims over several islets and shoals in the South China Sea.

In February, he said he was open to bilateral negotiations with China over the possibility of joint exploration of the Spratlys, echoing Beijing's line. He also said he might be willing to soften the Philippines' stance significantly — if China would build railroads in Bicol and in Mindanao. "Build us a railway just like the one you built in Africa, and let's set aside disagreements for a while," he said. Duterte was also skeptic about the Philippines' case at the tribunal, saying the ruling wouldn't be worth anything if China didn't comply with it. "I have a similar position as China's. I don't believe in solving the conflict through an international tribunal," he said. In April, he said he was ready to die to assert the country's claims over the disputed islands in the South China Sea but on the same breath, he said he would go to China and talk to its government if the latter refuses to comply with the decision of a UN arbitration tribunal hearing the Philippines' case against China.

Shortly after it became apparent that he would be proclaimed the next president of the Philippines, Duterte told US President Barack Obama over the phone that he would consider holding bilateral talks with China if efforts to resolve the dispute failed to progress. While Duterte assured Obama that he would continue with the mutual interests between the two longtime allies and that the Philippines would remain allied with the Western world on the South China Sea issue, he also told the US president that "if it (sea dispute) goes in still waters…there's no wind to move the sail, I might opt to go bilateral."

In another hint that the incoming administration would make a U-turn from President Aquino's hardline stance against the Chinese, including comparing Chinese President Xi Jin-ping to Nazi Germany's Adolf Hitler, Duterte described the Chinese leader "a great president."

In October 2014 shortly after the murder of Jennifer Laude by a US serviceman, Duterte said it would be better to scrap the Visiting Forces Agreement (VFA) and the Enhanced Defense Cooperation Agreement (EDCA) with the US if Filipinos cannot get justice in its own territory.

But two weeks ago, Duterte said he was in favor of continuing EDCA because "we don't have good external defense capabilities."

These pronouncements point to an inconsistent, unclear foreign policy vis-à-vis China and the US under the Duterte administration, and experts are worried that

Beijing could exploit this situation to gain advantage in the ongoing sea dispute.

For example, by saying that he would give Aquino's 'lawfare' strategy two years and if nothing happens, he would hold bilateral talks with China, he is playing right into China's hand and place the Philippines in the weak end of the negotiations. The Chinese would just continue with its arrogance and wait out the two years, knowing that they would get what they wanted shortly after.

The Philippines' efforts to push back on China have gained the backing of most of ASEAN countries, US, Japan, European Union and the G-7 leaders, who are in recent weeks doubling their efforts to pressure China into submitting to the decision of the UN tribunal. The decision is expected to come within the next few weeks.

With the increasing tension in the South China Sea, which has led to the rapid militarization of the region, the conflict could easily escalate from a shouting war to a shooting war.

In late May, the G-7 leaders sent a strong message to China. "We are concerned about the situation in the East and South China Seas, and emphasize the fundamental importance of peaceful management and settlement of disputes," the G7 leaders said.

They said claims in the East and South China Seas should be made based on international law and countries should refrain from "unilateral actions that could increase tensions" while also avoiding "force or coercion in trying to drive their claims."

China retorted that the G-7 leaders should stop hyping the territorial disputes in the South China Sea, saying the arbitration case brought by the Philippines is the root cause of the instability in the region. Chinese state media bluntly told the G-t leaders to stop meddling in the regional disputes.

Calling the Philippines' arbitration case just a show, Beijing warned "it will take a strong position in response" once the Philippines and its military allies use force in enforcing the ruling.

In Singapore over the weekend, Rear Adm. Guan Youfei, director of the foreign affairs office of China's national defense ministry, reiterated China would ignore the decision of the international arbitration panel in the Philippines' lawsuit.

As Duterte shows vacillation in his China stand, Beijing has been emboldened to continue its military buildup in the region through its artificial islands. US patrols observed Chinese vessels surveying the disputed Scarborough Shoal (Panatag Shoal) for another possible reclamation project.

Scarborough Shoal is just 120 nautical miles off the coast of Zambales and just 200 nautical miles from Manila. It is around 470 nautical miles from the closest point on the Chinese mainland.

US Defense Secretary Ashton Carter warned in Singapore on Saturday that Chinese construction in the disputed shoal would prompt "actions being taken" by the US and other nations. Carter said Beijing risks building a "Great

Wall of self-isolation" with its military expansion in the contested waters.

Rear Adm. Guan Youfei, who heads the Chinese office of international military cooperation, quickly attacked Carter's remarks, telling journalists they reflected a "Cold War mentality."

The US has backed its warnings with a recent show of force in the disputed sea, including the recent visit by the US Carrier Strike Group 3 and regular patrols by US fighter jets over the area.

With the rapid militarization in the South China Sea, the incoming administration has to make clear where it stands in the raging conflict between China and the US and its allies. After all, the Philippines' sovereignty and security depend so much on the outcome of the dispute.

The Philippines cannot afford to be caught in the middle of nowhere when the powder keg that has been floating on the South China Sea explodes.

Ooooo

24
Will somebody tell him campaign is over?
June 4, 2016

"SHUT UP!" Davao City Mayor Rodrigo Duterte uttered these words at least three times during the presidential campaign and in his daily press conferences since it became obvious he would be the next president of the Philippines.

The tough-talking mayor told both the US and Australian ambassadors to shut up when the diplomats of the country's two biggest allies criticized him for his remarks on the murder and rape of an Australian missionary. That was during a campaign in the Visayas. He said the diplomats were not Filipino citizens and should stay out of politics.

When told that women's groups had filed a complaint before the Commission on Human Rights (CHR) over his rape joke, he said he was just exercising his constitutional rights and could not be sued over his remarks.

And yet, when some soldiers exercised their constitutional right to free speech when they expressed concern over his plan to forge a peace deal with communist rebels and free all political prisoners, Duterte told them to shut up and be good soldiers.

When the CHR passed a resolution condemning him for his rape remarks, he told CHR Chairman Chit Gascon to shut up, adding that Gascon was "too naïve" and was an "idiot."

In January 2014, he had also told then CHR Chair Loretta Ann Rosales to shut up and not talk about what is ethical and unethical when it comes to fighting rice smuggling in the country. Rosales had criticized Duterte for saying he would kill anyone who smuggles rice in his city.

While Duterte loves to criticize and foul-mouth almost anybody that does not share his ideas of governance, he is quick to tell critics to shut up. And that's what's many people are worried about – a national leader who can't take criticisms and rattles recklessly when a touchy issue is raised against him.

This came again to the fore last week when asked about media killings during a press conference in Davao city. Instead of denouncing these killings, Duterte blurted out expletives and justified the murder of some media men, blaming corruption in the media and irresponsible reporting for the slayings.

"It's not because you're a journalist you're exempted from assassination if you're a son of a bitch," he added. Duterte said the freedom of expression enshrined in the 1987 Constitution would not protect reporters from assassination if they are corrupt or careless in reporting.

"The Constitution can no longer help you pag binaboy mo isang tao. Your freedom of expression can't help you if you've done something wrong with the guy," Duterte said. "… Most of those killed, to be frank, have done something. You won't be killed if you don't do anything wrong."

At one point during the press conference, Duterte, apparently irritated by a barrage of questions from the media, said: "May sundalo ba rito? I-Armalite nga mga ito."

It could have been a joke, but his statement justifying the killings of corrupt media members is an affront to freedom of expression and sends a chilling effect on journalists all over the country, corrupt or not. Who's to decide who are corrupt and who are not? The government officials being criticized? What will stop an irate official from claiming the journalist he had ordered killed was corrupt and from planting evidence before killing him?

Many media members who expressed support for Duterte are now regretting doing so. He had promised to pass the Freedom of Information (FOI) bill, and yet sends a mixed signal with his recent tirade against media men.

The international outrage followed his statement that corrupt journalists were legitimate targets of assassination. Duterte cited the case of Jun Pala, a journalist and politician who was murdered in Davao in 2003. Gunmen on a motorcycle gunned down Pala, who was a vocal critic of Duterte. His murder has never been solved.

"The example here is Pala. I do not want to diminish his memory but he was a rotten son of a bitch. He deserved it."

The justice department should reopen the case of Pala's murder since based on Duterte's statement, a possible motive has been established.

Now, it would appear that the murders of media members in the Philippines would remain unsolved for the next six years with the incoming president basically telling law enforcement authorities there is no need to investigate them as the victims most probably deserved being killed.

Duterte recklessly and insensitively tainted the memories of some 175 media members who have been killed since 1986, when democracy and freedom were supposedly restored with the ouster of President Marcos. This has outraged media groups all over the world.

Ryan Rosuaro, head of the National Union of Journalists of the Philippines, said, "It is appalling that President-elect Rodrigo Duterte should justify the murder of journalists in the country by playing the corruption card." The Foreign Correspondents Association of the Philippines said, "Duterte's statement is a chilling reminder that journalists in the Philippines continue to live under threat, decades after (the association) was founded to fight for press freedom at the height of Ferdinand Marcos's dictatorship."

International media monitor the Committee to Protect Journalists joined the condemnation, saying the only way to address the "woefully" high number of unresolved murders was through the courts.

"President-Elect Rodrigo Duterte's shocking remarks apparently excusing extrajudicial killings threaten to make the Philippines into a killing field for journalists," it said in a statement. "We strongly urge him to retract his comments and to signal that he intends to protect, not target, the press."

But will the incoming president even listen? Apparently not.

When told that the international media group Reporters Without Borders is calling for a boycott of his press conferences, Duterte blurted: "I was saying, you idiots, do not threaten me. I said I'm ready to lose the presidency, my honor or my life. Just do not fuck with me."

Duterte laid down his classification of journalists: the "crusaders, who bare all to the public," the "mouthpiece of vested interests," and "the lowlives."

Duterte's apologists tried to come to his rescue.

Designated presidential spokesperson Salvador Panelo said Duterte's statement on the killings of journalists was "taken out of context, misinterpreted and misunderstood."

How can the statement be taken out of context? It was televised live on TV, witnessed by millions.

Senator Aquilino "Koko" Pimentel III, president of Duterte's party PDP-Laban, on the other hand, appealed to the public not to "misinterpret" the statement of President-elect Rodrigo Duterte that corruption is the root cause of media killings in the country.

"Do not mistake or misinterpret the statement of the President. Ang sinabi lang naman ng Presidente, we have freedom of the press but we also have to be responsible in exercising it and given the nature of the Filipinos, sometimes they resort to violence and the Constitution can't protect you from violence," Pimentel said in an interview at the Senate.

If Duterte had said it that way, there would have been no outrage. But no, he had to call media men "sons of bitches," "lowlives," the mouthpiece of vested interests," etc.

"We need a little understanding. He does not have any bad intention," Vitaliano Aguirre II, Duterte's designated justice secretary, said. "He uses hyperbole to attract attention to what he wants to say… He intentionally exaggerates, like during the campaign. You have to give him some leeway… so his statements can be interpreted so that it could be toned down."

I have one advice to Duterte's advisers. Tell him to "shut up" and just wait for his inauguration as the 16th president of this country. No more press conferences from Davao. No more expletives. Just be sincere in uniting the country and in fighting crime and corruption. After all, the campaign is over. He is already the president-elect.

Ooooo

25
Why I Publish/Reprint Books

Tatay Jobo Elizes
Self-Publisher

Writings are timeless and they act as mirrors to history. I publish writings as they remain relevant anytime. I have seen a lot of good writings in the internet, in magazines and newspapers. But most writers have only one or two articles and therefore not enough material to be published as a book. And yet, many of them need to be published or archived. There are also writers who write a lot but never publish them. There are also old books with no more prints available. The solution is to publish/reprint.

I do this for free because of the print-books-on-demand (POD) system, but the printed or hardcopy is not free

The printed book will always be there among your collections or libraries. Not all use the internet.

The internet access has its technical problems. I can produce fiction, non-fiction, in color also.

My booklist can be seen at http://tinyurl.com/mj76ccq (copy and paste)

Permission had been granted by the author/authors to print their books under my free self-publishing service. They own copyrights to their works.

Interested reader may request free reading of any of my books, articles or essays via online reading or ebook. Just select and email me.

Thank you.

ooooo

www.ingramcontent.com/pod-product-compliance
Lightning Source LLC
Chambersburg PA
CBHW070814240726

48654CB00007B/341